they called her

Miriam

the virgin of nazareth

Victor Buksbazen
The Friends of Israel Gospel Ministry, Inc.
Bellmawr, NJ

They Called Her Miriam: The Virgin of Nazareth

Original copyright © 1963 under the title *Miriam: The Virgin of Nazareth* by The Spearhead Press, a division of The Friends of Israel Gospel Ministry, Inc., Bellmawr, NJ 08099

Reedited in 2017 by The Friends of Israel.

Copyright © 2017 by The Friends of Israel Gospel Ministry, Inc. Bellmawr, NJ 08099

For information, contact The Friends of Israel Gospel Ministry, Inc., P.O. Box 908, Bellmawr, NJ 08099.

Library of Congress Catalog Card Number: 2017952336

ISBN-13 978-0-915540-90-7

Cover by Catie Perseo.

Visit our website at foi.org

Acknowledgments

The making of a book is not unlike the building of a house. The plan must first be conceived in the mind of the architect or of the author— the labor and the painstaking numerous details must be carried out by capable and willing hands.

We take this opportunity of expressing our thanks to all those whose labor, counsel, and encouragement have contributed substantially to the completion of this study.

We are grateful to the publishers who have granted us permission to quote from their works; to my former secretary, Miss Elsie R. Snyder, for her labor of love in typing and re-typing the manuscript; to Miss Mary Bennett, PhD, for reading the manuscript and for making some valuable suggestions; to Miss Lillian Balistocky who was kind enough to prepare the general index of subjects and also the list of scriptural references.

Last, but not least, I am deeply grateful to my dear wife, Lydia, who has given so much of her time, her strength, and encouragement to make this book possible.

"For He that is mighty hath done to me great things; and holy is His Name," Luke 1:49.

CONTENTS

PREFACE

Comparatively little has been written about the virgin mother of our Lord by Protestant scholars. This is due in part to the fact that the Church of Rome has, in the course of time, transformed the radiant, scriptural personality of Mary into a semi-pagan deity, and has directly or indirectly encouraged the honoring, and in practice the worship of her to such an extent that Mary has almost replaced her Son in the devotions of many Catholics.

As a reaction to this idolatrous practice, evangelical Christians have by and large shied away from the subject of Mary.

Another reason why Protestants have written comparatively little about Mary is the paucity of reliable historical material concerning her life and person.

The fact is that, outside of what the New Testament, particularly the Gospels, tells us about Mary, we know practically nothing about her. It is quite evident that the Gospels were not written with a view to providing us with a detailed story of the life of Jesus, but rather "that ye might believe that Jesus is the Christ, the Son of God, and that believing ye might have life through his name" (Jn. 20:31). Even less has the New Testament provided us with records concerning the life of His mother.

This being the situation, we can hardly be expected to write a life of the virgin mother even in mere outline.

The traditions and legends which came into existence in post-apostolic times are so unreliable and often so fanciful that these can hardly be considered a serious source of historical information.

We shall therefore confine ourselves chiefly to the New Testament for data relating to Mary. However, we will use for our study those historical sources for some supplementary and background information which we may find useful. Even with the aid of all these additional sources it would still be all but impossible to draw an outline of the life of Mary. Nevertheless, from the available data we hope to gain some insight into the life of the one who was God's chosen vessel to give birth to the Messiah of Israel and the Savior of the world.

The Old Testament Apocrypha and the Talmud have a good deal

to tell us about Jewish life in Galilee of that period. This should help us to understand better those forces which were at work long before and during her lifetime, influencing and molding her lovely personality. But to attempt the task of presenting her life story would be just as impossible as an attempt to paint her physical appearance, concerning which we know nothing. Where God Himself has chosen to be silent, we dare not speak. However, we hope that our study may help us sketch with very light strokes the outlines of the personality of the one who was the "handmaiden of the Lord," chosen by God to be the mother of the Messiah.

We shall attempt to present her life on the canvas of her native Galilee, and against the historical background of her times and the spiritual climate in which she lived.

Such a drawing, deficient and incomplete as it must perforce be, we trust will serve to increase, even in some small measure, our knowledge of her who belongs to the great heroes of faith, and should help to restore to her rightful place of honor one of those singularly beautiful and saintly women in whom the pages of the Old and New Testaments abound.

It is also our earnest desire that in gaining a glimpse of the true Mary of Scripture we may help to overcome those fables and deceptions which were built up around her by pagan hands and minds, and which have replaced in the hearts of many her blessed Son, Jesus, with the image of an ancient pagan deity. In so doing, we shall be serving in some small measure the cause of Him who said, "Ye shall know the truth and the truth shall make you free."

A word of explanation is due concerning the title of this study, *Miriam the Virgin of Nazareth.*

Why do we call her "Miriam" instead of "Mary," as she has always been known among Christians? We do it for two reasons:

Miriam was her true biblical name in Hebrew. *Mary* is the modern English version of the name Miriam. The original name-bearer of Miriam was the sister of Moses. The Septuagint rendered this name in Greek *Mariam.* The Greek New Testament also called the name of the virgin mother Mariam. The Latin translation called her *Maria.* It was from Latin that her name entered into all European languages and, in due course, assumed the English form of "Mary."

We shall use the name Mary when quoting Scripture or other sources, just as she is named in those sources.

But since we are trying to find the real Mary, as presented to us in the Scriptures, we shall therefore revert to her true and original Hebrew name and call her Miriam. In this way we shall seek to emphasize her biblical and historical background and the fact that the mother of our Lord was like her blessed Son, Jewish.

There is another reason why we prefer "Miriam" to "Mary." The name *Mary* has today become so deeply imbedded in the dogmas and the worship of the Roman Church that, whenever her name is mentioned, all kinds of confusing associations spring to mind. We do not want Miriam, the wonderful virgin mother of our Savior, confused with the alien image of Mary of Roman doctrines.

Miriam, the blessed Jewish maiden of Nazareth, and Mary of Rome have little or nothing in common. This study is a humble and inadequate attempt to remove some of the paint and varnish which perhaps well-meaning, but scripturally ill-tutored and semi-pagan minds have superimposed upon her lovely human personality, of which we are granted only a few glimpses in the New Testament.

INTRODUCTION

EVALUATION OF SOURCES

"I am thinking and wondering," laments Thomas of Villanova (1488-1556),

> *why the Evangelists deal so fully with John the Baptist and the other apostles and so meagerly with the Virgin Mary who is above them all through the dignity of her life. Why, I say, has it not been handed down to us how she was conceived, how she was born, how she was brought up, with what virtue she was adorned or what she did with her Son in human relationships, how she was accustomed to conduct herself with him or how she lived with the apostles after the Ascension? These were great matters and worthy of being remembered, of being read devoutly by the faithful, of being meditated on by the people. O Evangelists, I say, why do you deprive us of such joy by your silence? Why are you silent about things so happy, desirable and joyful?*[1]

This cry expresses in a dramatic way the perplexity and frustration of a Marian devotee who would dearly have loved to have more details concerning the life of Mary, the subject of his devotion. What is known about Miriam is contained in the few meager New Testament data. Everything else is unfortunately of questionable authenticity or reliability. However, where facts were not available, the imagination of men more than made up for such lack.

In the early centuries a vast literature came into being which purported to fill the gap of our knowledge concerning the life of the mother of our Lord and of other New Testament personalities.

This vast literature of the first three centuries has come to be known as the apocryphal New Testament, or writings which were not included in the canon or the accepted list of the New Testament books.

THE NEW TESTAMENT CANON

The Greek word *canon* means literally "rod," then "order" or "rule." The canon of the New Testament came into being by a process of approval of those writings which were of apostolic origin, and of elimination of those which were not. The Gospels and the epistles were at first read in the various Christian assemblies. Those which carried the character of authenticity and apostolic origin were approved by the early churches. For a time there existed differences of opinion concerning some of the New Testament writings. However, toward the end of the second century the New Testament canon was well established. Later synods put the seal of their approval upon an already established New Testament canon.

Numerous writings, which did not have the marks of authenticity, or were not in harmony with the spirit and the contents of the accepted New Testament writings, were rejected as spurious.

Some of these spurious or questionable writings, often attributed to apostles or evangelists by unknown scribes, were preserved and came down to us in Greek, Latin, Coptic, Syriac, or Arabic. Other documents were consigned to oblivion and eventually disappeared.

These extra-canonical writings are known by the general designation of the apocryphal New Testament. They contain much of that which is fanciful, legendary, or unworthy of our Lord. The Greek term *apocryphal* means hidden or mysterious. Later the word came to mean "spurious," or that which is not authentic.

One must admire the wisdom of the early Christians and their sound judgment in rejecting these spurious documents. Living much closer to the events and persons described in the New Testament, they were able to differentiate between that which was authentic and that which was questionable.

The New Testament books compare with those apocryphal writings as dime store diamonds with the genuine article.

And yet, though fantastic and fanciful, some of these extra-canonical documents may contain some elements of truth preserved in early traditions. It is interesting to note that some of the apocryphal documents come close to some of our New Testament writings. For instance, the Gospel according to the Hebrews is similar to the Gospel of Matthew.

Other so-called Gospels (of which there are about 50), epistles, and acts of various apostles purporting to be the records of the apostles or the original evangelists contain some elements which may be based on early traditions current among the Christians of that time. Our real difficulty is how to establish where the element of truth is, and where legend and vivid imagination have taken over.

The apocryphal writings abound in details concerning the infancy and early life of our Lord, also about Joseph and Mary, about her death and ascension to heaven. Some purport to contain sayings of the Lord Jesus not related in the New Testament. It is quite obvious that these writings cannot serve us as a mine of dependable historical material. The early church wisely rejected these apocryphal writings.

The Old Testament Apocrypha, which give us an insight into the life and thought of the Jewish people before Christ, are of greater importance to us than the New Testament Apocrypha. Yet before we can discuss the Old Testament Apocrypha it is necessary to consider briefly the origin and significance of the Old Testament canon.

Although the term *canon* is Greek, its meaning as a collection of God-inspired sacred books is of Jewish origin and probably goes back to the middle of the fifth century, BC to the days of Ezra and Nehemiah.

The purpose of the Old Testament canon is two-fold:

1. To include certain sacred books in the Bible.
2. To exclude those books which did not belong there.

The first reference to a collection of sacred books is found in Daniel 9:2. "In the first year of his reign, I Daniel understood by books the number of the years."

These "books" were later referred to in rabbinical literature as *sifrei hakodesh*, that is, "holy books." The same term was used in the New Testament: "Which he had promised afore by his prophets in the holy scriptures"(Rom. 1:2).

By contrast all secular or extra-canonical books were referred to as *sifrei chitzonin* which means "outside books."

The Hebrew Scriptures (Old Testament) were divided into three sections: the Law, the Prophets, and the Writings.[2]

The Hebrew abbreviation for this three-fold division of the Old Testament is commonly known as the Tenakh (*Torah, Neviim, Ketubim*).

Jewish tradition ascribes the collection of the Old Testament books into one sacred canon to Nehemiah (2 Maccabees 2: 13–15), or to Ezra the Scribe (5th century BC).

Ancient Jewish scholars assumed the divine inspiration of every book in the Old Testament and of every word in them. The authorship of various books was ascribed to various prophets. There was perfect agreement among them as to the non-canonical character of the apocryphal books. These they considered as edifying but not inspired.

To Jesus, the Old Testament was the Bible, the infallible Word of God. He accepted its divine inspiration and canonicity without any reservation and often quoted from the Old Testament as prophetic of Himself: "Search the scriptures; for in them ye think ye have eternal life: and they are they which testify of me" (Jn. 5:39).

The term *Old Testament* did not come into being until after the New Testament writings were collected into one universally recognized canon among Christians. Significantly, Christ never quoted or mentioned by name any of the apocryphal writings which were so numerous in His times.[3]

THE OLD TESTAMENT APOCRYPHA

Much older than the apocryphal New Testament were the Old Testament Apocrypha. These are the religious writings which came into existence during the period between the two Testaments. The Jews, for good reasons, refused to include the Apocrypha in the Old Testament. But the Roman Catholic Church later included them in their version of the Old Testament.

The Church of Rome believed to find, in these apocryphal writings, support for certain of her doctrine. For instance, the doctrine of merit acquired through good works is based on Tobit 12:9.[4] Likewise the doctrine of purgatory and the efficacy of prayers offered up for the dead were based on a passage from the book of 2 Maccabees.[5]

Jerome, the fourth-century Bible translator and scholar who knew Hebrew well, declared unreservedly that books which were outside the Hebrew canon should not be ranked as canonical. In his Latin translation of the Bible known as the Vulgate, he separated carefully those which were canonical or generally accepted Scriptures from the non-canonical books or the Apocrypha.

The Old Testament Apocypha contain much of Jewish beliefs, wisdom, history, hopes, and expectations between the close of the Old Testament period and the birth of Christ. Many of the historical events described in the Old Testament Apocrypha find confirmation in the secular sources of that period.

Thus, these Apocrypha form a bridge between the Old and New Testaments, and give us an insight into the life and thought of the Jewish people during these intervening four centuries.

By studying the Apocrypha the student of early Christianity gains a more complete understanding of the political, social, and religious forces and of the spiritual climate in which the Jews of that time lived. The Apocrypha reflect the Messianic hope and yearnings of the Jews which were so intense at that time.

The Old Testament Apocrypha provide the background for our study.

JOSEPHUS

Another very important, although not always completely reliable source of information for this period is Josephus, the Jewish historian of the first century AD, who gives us a detailed picture of the history of the Jews from the earliest times, and especially during the first century until the destruction of the Temple in AD 70. Josephus was a younger contemporary of Christ. He was not only an historian but, like Sir Winston Churchill many centuries later, was himself an actor who played an important part in history which he wrote.[6]

THE DEAD SEA SCROLLS

Since 1947 a vast new literature, as yet not fully explored or evaluated, has come to light. These are the now-famous Dead Sea Scrolls which are related to the "Zadokite Documents," found some 50 years ago among a collection of discarded old manuscripts in a Cairo synagogue.

The Dead Sea Scrolls, while not containing definite historical data which could add to our knowledge of New Testament events, nevertheless, help us to understand more clearly the spiritual climate which prevailed among a considerable segment of the Jewish people at the turn of the era.

The Dead Sea Scrolls provide us with an insight into the life, practices, and beliefs of the ascetic Jewish sect known as the community of Qumran on the northern shores of the Dead Sea. Their highly disciplined and monastic way of life apparently came to a violent end in the year AD 68, when the Tenth Roman Legion entered the area and destroyed their communal center at Qumran.

Of special importance to us among the Dead Sea Scrolls are the

Manual of Discipline, and the collection of Psalms of Thanksgiving.

The members of this wilderness community of Qumran apparently considered themselves as the true congregation of Israel, the Sons of Light, the faithful remnant who were loyal to God's covenant, and were waiting eagerly for the coming of the "prophet like unto Moses" spoken of in Deuteronomy 18:15–18.

This prophet was to be the Messiah who would usher in the golden age, when the knowledge of God should cover the earth as the waters cover the sea. For them the Kingdom of heaven was indeed at hand.

It is interesting to note that John the Baptist came from the desert beyond Jordan, from an area where presumably this group lived.

The Dead Sea Scrolls give us a good insight into the religious ideas and an understanding of the spiritual forces at work among the group of some 4,000 Jewish "come outers," who went out into the wilderness to live a holy and separated life.

Like some of the Gospel personalities associated with the birth of Jesus, they were awaiting with great intensity "the consolation of Israel" which would usher in the Kingdom of God under the reign of God's Anointed One, the Messiah. [7]

MIRIAM IN THE QUR'AN

Although in the early centuries much was written by Christians about the mother of Jesus, these writings were largely products of piety or fantasy which add little or nothing to our historical understanding of the New Testament Miriam. However, the views and beliefs of Christians in the first centuries have had considerable influence on the Arabs and to some extent on the Jews of that period. Muhammad, the founder of Islam in the seventh century, in his travels as an Arab merchant and later as a religious innovator, came in contact with many Jews and Christians. Much of what he learned from them, often distorted and misunderstood, was later incorporated in the Qur'an, the "Bible" of the Muslims. There are a number of references to Jesus and to Miriam in the Qur'an. [8] At best, these passages of the Qur'an reflect some of the views by certain sectarian groups of Christians during the times of Muhammad.

THE TALMUD

In the Talmud, that vast storehouse of biblical commentaries, legal discussions, traditions, historical records, fables, and Jewish folklore which came into existence in the first five centuries of the Christian era, there are a number of references to Jesus and His mother, most of them unfavorable.

After the "conversion" of Constantine the Great in the fourth century, the Jews lived in countries where Christianity was the dominant religion which, under the influence of a hostile church, was contemptuous of the Jews. Unable to pay back their oppressors in kind, the Jews assuaged their hurt by ridiculing or misrepresenting the founder of Christianity. A subject which often came under their hostile attention was His virgin birth. Thus Jesus was referred to as Yeshu the son of Pandera. *Yeshu* is in all probability an unfriendly nickname of the Hebrew name *Yeshua*—Jesus, while *Pandera* is probably a mocking rendition of the Greek word *parthenos*—a virgin. There is of course difference of opinion as to the real meaning of above terms. [9]

In all the vast literature referred to above we would look in vain for reliable historical data relating directly to the life of Mary or Jesus. Nevertheless all these writings, particularly the Old Testament Apocrypha and the earlier parts of the Talmud, the Mishna, are most valuable in helping us to understand the religious life, the laws and customs of the Jews, their hopes and beliefs during that vital period under our study.

EARLY CHRISTIANITY IN CONTEMPORARY JEWISH THOUGHT

For hundreds of years the subject of Christianity and its origin were forbidden territory to the Jews. Jesus was referred to as "that Man" or "the Hanged One." Cruel and harsh treatment alienated the Jews and embittered them against Christianity. With the dawn of more friendly relations between Jews and Christians, the subject of Jesus has increasingly become an absorbing intellectual pursuit among the Jews. Professor Joseph Klausner (1874-1958), of the Hebrew University in Jerusalem, wrote an exhaustive study about the life of Jesus and also of the apostle Paul. [10]

Sholem Asch, a Jewish writer of unusual skill and keen sensitivity, had a deep appreciation for the Person of Jesus whom he considered as the Savior of the nations, whom God sent with a special mission to bring light to the Gentiles. He wrote three novels dealing with early Christianity: *The Nazarene, The Apostle,* and *Mary.* In the last, Sholem Asch gave a tender portrayal of the mother of Jesus, beautiful, alive, but at times bordering on the fantastic. His Mary makes pleasant and stimulating reading. However, it has little value from the standpoint of biblical research.

Such, in brief, is the vast material for the study of Miriam and her times; and yet it is very limited in reliable information. This is not enough to give us a portrait of the mother of Jesus, yet it may perhaps help us to sketch with light pencil strokes an imaginative outline of the beautiful life and saintly personality of Miriam, the greatest contribution Jewish womanhood has made to humanity's gallery of great women.

PART ONE

The World in Which Miriam Lived

CHAPTER ONE

The Political Background

Ever since Jerusalem fell to the Babylonians in 586 BC, and the Temple was destroyed, Israel has had no real independence. There were periods of comparative independence, but only as feudal vassals of foreign overlords.

The Babylonian supremacy over Palestine lasted from 587-539 BC, when, in turn, Babylon was conquered by Cyrus of Persia, referred to in Isaiah 44:28; 45:1; Ezra 1:1; 4:3.

Cyrus the Great was unique in his tolerance toward conquered peoples. He caused to be engraved on a cylinder:

> *My numerous troops advanced into the heart of Babylon peaceably....In Babylon and all the outlying regions I strove for peace.... The yoke which was not honorable I removed from them. Their run-down houses I repaired....The gods...I caused to return, their hearts to their places I returned and caused to dwell in an eternal habitation. All their people I assembled and I returned to their habitations.*[1]

The Persian period of supremacy over Palestine lasted about 200 years, from 539 to 336 BC.

EZRA THE SCRIBE

It was during this period that a man of unusual stature arose among the Jews who left his imprint upon Judaism as few others have. In fact, he may be considered the father of historic Judaism. His name was Ezra the Scribe, a man of priestly descent. It was he who caused the Old Testament, hitherto preserved in the old Hebrew characters, to be written in the square Hebrew script used among the Jews to the present day. The greatest Bible scholar of his day, Ezra presided over a group of learned men, known as the Men of the Great Assembly, whose task it was to interpret biblical law and observances, and their practical application in daily life. He was the forerunner of the later scribes who were biblical scholars.

In the year 457 BC, Ezra led the second group of repatriates from Babylon to Jerusalem. In all there were three deportations from Palestine to Babylon and also three returns:

First deportation to Babylon in 605 BC.

Second deportation in 597 BC.

Third deportation in 586 BC.

First return to Palestine under Sheshbazzar in 538 BC.

Second return under Ezra in 457 BC.

Third return under Nehemiah in 445 BC.

Ezra and Nehemiah were jointly responsible for a religious revival among the Jews and the rebuilding of Jerusalem.

However, the impact of Ezra upon his people was by far the more lasting, and its effect endures even to the present day.

THE PTOLEMIES AND THE SELEUCIDS

In the year 335 BC, a new star arose on the political horizon of the Hellenistic world which shone brightly but briefly. The star was Alexander the Great of Macedonia. He, too, was kindly disposed towards the Jews. After his death in 323 BC, his empire was divided between his generals. Syria, of which Palestine was a province, became the dominion of Seleucus, and Ptolemy became ruler of Egypt. Both generals established dynasties named after them.

In consequence of this, Palestine became a province of the Syrian Empire of the Seleucids, who sought to Hellenize their dominions, forcing upon the Jewish people Greek customs, religion, and art. These attempts were violently resented by the Jews, especially by the pious and nationally minded Pharisees and by other religious leaders.

THE MACCABEES

Antiochus IV, known as Epiphanes the Illustrious, was particularly vicious and ruthless in his efforts to Hellenize Palestine. In 165 BC, he defiled the Temple in Jerusalem and forced the sacrifice of a pig to Zeus on the altar of Jehovah and forbade circumcision or the observance of the Sabbath. All this precipitated a religious revolt, led by the priest Judas, surnamed the Maccabee (the Hammer), and by his five stalwart sons.[2]

The period of the Maccabees and their successors known also as the Hasmoneans was a time of relative independence for the Jewish nation. Nevertheless Palestine continued under Syrian overlordship. The Hasmonean dynasty lasted from 165 to 40 BC, when the last Hasmonean high priest-king, Antigonous, was succeeded by the Idumean Antipater, who was appointed by Rome as procurator of Judea. Antipater was the father of Herod, so-called the Great.

At first, the sons of Judas Maccabeus jealously guarded the national independence and the integrity of the religious life of the Jews. But under their successors a moral and spiritual decline ensued. The Hasmonean rulers, who combined religious as well as political power, gradually became infected with the foreign ways and the idolatry of the surrounding peoples. Some of them were guilty of unheard-of cruelty.[3]

The high priesthood became the object of bargaining, the sacred office sometimes going to the highest bidder. It was a tragic irony that the Hasmonean dynasty, which started out as a revolt against idolatry and foreign rule, in the end succumbed to alien ways and culture. As a result of this, the Hasmoneans lost the support of the common people and, above all, the now-powerful movement of the Pharisees and scribes. The Hasmoneans, like most of the priestly clan, were Sadducees religiously, who favored a friendly *modus vivendi* with the Syrian and later with the Roman powers.

ROMAN INTERVENTION

During one of the fratricidal quarrels among the Hasmonean princes, which involved the high priesthood and the royal succession, Rome was invited as an arbiter. The results of this intervention were fatal to Jewish independence. In 63 BC, the Roman general Pompey invaded Palestine on the invitation of one of the quarreling parties. He took Jerusalem and desecrated the Temple. From then on, the Hasmoneans were rulers only by the grace of Rome, which wielded actual power. The last Hasmonean ruler, Antigonous, was murdered in 40 BC, by the Idumean half-Jew, Herod, known as the Great. A shrewd and ruthless man, through intrigues with Rome, he was able to establish the Herodian dynasty, which began in 40 BC, and outlived the destruction of the Temple in AD 70.

The most famous of the Herodians was this Herod the Great, who ruled from 40-4 BC. His reign was characterized by unheard-of extravagance, oppression of the people, cruelty, dissolute living, and murder of his nearest kin. According to Josephus, in the days of Herod no woman's honor and no man's life was safe. The victims of Herod included his most beloved wife (he had 10 of them), Mariamne, father's brother, three of his own sons, and many of the surviving Hasmonean princelings who might conceivably have had any claims to the throne of Judea.

One of Herod's all-consuming passions was the building of magnificent cities, lavish palaces, and imposing monuments. This he did in order to perpetuate his name. He built the magnificent port of Caesarea, in honor of Caesar. He rebuilt ancient Shechem in Samaria and named it Sebaste, after Caesar Augustus. He rebuilt and greatly enhanced the Temple in Jerusalem with the dual purpose of pleasing the Jews and perpetuating his own memory. These were only a few of the lavish projects which he undertook and which cost the nation incredible amounts of money and labor.

Rome, Athens, Corinth, Antioch, and many other foreign capitals also benefited from Herod's wasteful generosity. To accomplish all this and to keep up his lavish and dissolute court, and to provide extravagant gifts for various rulers and potentates, Herod bled his country dry. Because of all this, Herod the Great was probably one of the most hated rulers of the Jews in all their history.

Here is how the famous first-century Jewish historian Josephus, who prided himself on being an objective chronicler, characterized Herod:

> *Now some there are who stand amazed at the diversity of Herod's nature and purposes; for when we have respect to his magnificence, and the benefits which he bestowed on all mankind, there is no possibility for even those who had the least respect for him to deny, or not openly to confess, that he had a nature vastly beneficent; but when any one looks upon the punishments he inflicted, and the injuries he did, not only to his subjects but to his nearest relations, and takes notice of his severe and unrelenting disposition there, he*

will be forced to allow that he was brutish, and a stranger to all humanity: insomuch that these men suppose his nature to be different, and sometimes in contradiction with itself; but I am myself of another opinion, and imagine that the occasion of both these sorts of actions was one and the same; for being a man ambitious of honour, and quite overcome by that passion, he was induced to be magnificent, wherever there appeared any hopes of a future memorial, or of reputation at present; and as his expenses were beyond his abilities, he was necessitated to be harsh to his subjects; for the persons on whom he expended his money were so many, that they made him very bad procurer of it; and because he was conscious that he was hated by those under him, for the injuries he did them, he thought it not an easy thing to amend his offences, for that was inconvenient for his revenue; he therefore strove on the other side to make their ill-will an occasion of his gains.

As to his own court, therefore, if any one was not very obsequious to him in his language, and would not confess himself to be his slave, or but seemed to think of any innovation in his government, he was not able to contain himself, but prosecuted his very kindred and friends, and punished them as if they were enemies; and this wickedness undertook out of a desire that he might be himself alone honoured.

Now for this my assertion about that passion of his, we have the greatest evidence, by what he did to honour Caesar and Agrippa, and his other friends; for with what honours he paid his respects to them who were his superiors, the same did he desire to be paid to himself; and what he thought the most excellent present he could make another, he discovered an inclination to have the like presented to himself; but now the Jewish nation is by their law a stranger to all such things, and accustomed to prefer righteousness to glory; for which reason that nation was not agreeable to him, because it was out of their power to flatter the king's ambition with statues or temples, or any other such performances: and this seems to me to have been at once the occasion of Herod's crimes as to his own courtiers and counsellors, and of his benefactors as to foreigners and those that had no relation to him. [4]

From the above testimony and from everything else we know about
Herod "the Great," it is evident that the story of the Slaughter of the
Innocents, as recorded in the Gospel of Matthew 2:16–19, was quite
in keeping with the cruel and ruthless character of this man.

To crown his infamous life, before he died, Herod ordered the arrest
of a large number of the most prominent Jews from all of Palestine.
These were to be executed on the day of his death, so that there should
be no general rejoicing upon his demise. Fortunately, this bloodthirsty
order was not carried out by his son Archeleus and Herod's death was
celebrated as a national feast day after all.

After the death of Herod the Great, in 4 BC, probably March
12, Palestine was divided among his sons: Archeleus receiving Judea,
Samaria, and Idumea; Philip the eastern province of Jordan; and Herod
Antipas (from 4 BC through AD 39) became the ruler of Galilee and
Perea. Among the subjects of Herod Antipas was an impoverished
family in Nazareth, a man known as Joseph the carpenter, his wife
Miriam, and her son, Jesus.

The Herod mentioned in Acts 12 was Herod Agrippa I, grandson of
Herod the Great. He managed to obtain the rule over all of Palestine
and reigned between AD 40 and 44. The Herod of Acts 25 and 26 was
his son, Herod Agrippa II, and great-grandson of Herod the Great.
After the fall of Jerusalem in AD 70, he lived in Tiberias as a vassal of
Rome, and died in the year 100, the last scion of that cruel and wicked
dynasty of the Herods.

It was during the turbulent, bloodstained period seething with unrest
and with high hope, under Herod the Great, when many in Israel were
crying out to God in agony of soul for salvation, that Miriam became
the espoused wife of Joseph, and Christ was born in Bethlehem.

The birth of Christ indeed came to pass in "the fullness of time,"
when the cup of Israel's suffering and sorrow, of blood and tears was
full and running over.

CHAPTER TWO

Galilee in the Days of Christ

Galilee, the northern province of Palestine, was the ancient home of four tribes: Issachar, Zebulon, Naphtali, and Asher. The western borders of Galilee reached the Phoenician port city of Tyre, and of Syria to the northeast. On the south, the province of Galilee adjoined Samaria and the River Kishon.

Biblical Galilee was a rich land, fertile and densely populated. Josephus maintained that there were 240 towns and villages in Galilee. The smallest of these, he wrote, contained no less than 15,000 inhabitants. Although this was probably an exaggeration, undoubtedly Galilee was very populous (probably about 3 million people). This is how Josephus characterized the people and province of Galilee:

> With this limited area, and although surrounded by such powerful
> foreign nations, the two Galilees (Upper and Lower) have always
> resisted any hostile invasion, for the inhabitants are from infancy
> inured to war, and have at all times been numerous; never did the
> men lack courage nor the country men. For the land is everywhere
> so rich in soil and pasturage and produces such variety of trees,
> that even the most indolent are tempted by these facilities to devote
> themselves to agriculture. In fact, every inch of the soil has been cul-
> tivated by the inhabitants; there is not a parcel of waste land. The
> towns, too, are thickly distributed; and even the villages, thanks to
> the fertility of the soil, are all so densely populated that the smallest
> of them contains above fifteen thousand inhabitants.[1]

It was a land famous for olive trees. In fact, it has been said it was easier to raise a forest of olive trees in Galilee than one child in Judea.

This was the land where Asher "dipped his foot in oil" (Dt. 33:24). Here was also an abundance of fruit and grain, and a large variety of fish from the Sea of Galilee.

A contemporary saying had it, "If anyone wishes to be rich, let him go north, if he wants to be wise let him go south."[2]

Galilee was also famous for its industry: pottery, dye works, and shipbuilding. The great international highway from Egypt led through Caesarea along the Mediterranean coast across Galilee to Damascus. Nazareth therefore lay on the main road of international traffic and commerce. This town was also one of the priestly centers.[3] Here one of the 24 groups of priests, who ministered in the Temple, would gather together in order to go up to Jerusalem.

In addition to Nazareth there were such well-known cities as Sepphoris, the capital of Galilee; Capernaum, where Matthew later sat at the receipt of custom (Mt. 9:9); Bethsaida, "the House of Fishes," where Andrew and Peter were born (Jn. 1:44); Safad, "the City on a Hill" (Mt. 5:14), and the City of Tiberias, on the western shores of the Sea of Galilee, built shortly after the birth of Christ by Herod Antipas, the tetrarch of Galilee, and named after Emperor Tiberius. However, the rabbis forbade the Jews to inhabit the City of Tiberias because it was built on an ancient cemetery.

Frequent mingling with Gentiles, Greeks, Romans, Arabs ("Galilee of the Gentiles," Mt. 4:15) who lived in neighboring cities around Galilee or passed through their country, tended to make the Galileans more cosmopolitan and tolerant than their compatriots of Judea. The Galileans were a warmhearted, generous but impulsive and often pugnacious people. Many of the revolutions against foreign oppressors were sparked in Galilee. Peter was a rather typical Galilean as regards his temperament.

These hard working and practical Galileans were not too careful about rabbinical tradition, nor were they given to fine theological distinctions and hairsplitting. Their piety was of an inward and practical variety. Hot tempered, they were easily provoked to wrath.

The last two centuries before the destruction of the Temple, the Galileans were often involved in fratricidal strife against one another and in numerous revolts against the oppressive rule of Rome.[4] These violent outbursts bled the country dry, and heightened the yearning for a divine redeemer—the Messiah.

The Galileans' lack of schooling in the traditions of the elders made them at times the source of ridicule among the learned men of Judea, so that it was natural to make such remarks as "Can there any good thing come out of Nazareth?" (Jn. 1:46). Incidentally, all Galileans, because of their imperfect observance of the rabbinic rites and commandments, were considered ritually unclean.

The Galileans living in a land at best semi-Judaized, and so far from the Sanctuary, had never submitted fully to the Biblical laws concerning Levitical defilement. According to the letter of the Law they were all, like the Jews of today, permanently impure, and whatever they touched was defiled.[5]

Their rustic speech and peculiar pronunciation made them an easy target for contemptuous remarks.[6]

The language used in Galilee as in the rest of Palestine was, at that time, Aramaic. It was undoubtedly the language used by Jesus and His mother, Miriam. This is abundantly evident from the Gospel narratives (Mk. 5:41; 7:34). There is no direct proof that the Greek language was used in the home of Jesus. It thus becomes important when reading the Greek Gospels to try to think back to the original Aramaic words as they fell from the lips of Jesus or His disciples. Greek, however, was spoken by the educated classes and aristocracy. (An interesting attempt to reconstruct the original sayings of Christ from Greek into Aramaic was made by the biblical scholar Gustaf Dalmann, in his work *Jesus-Jeschua*, 1922.)

It may also be assumed that those who had frequent contact with foreigners, travelers, and with the authorities were acquainted with Greek, the common language of the Hellenist world.

PHARISEES, SADDUCEES, AND THE COMMON PEOPLE

In the latter part of the first century BC, the Pharisees, though few in number, became the most influential movement among the Jews. They were a closely knit religious fraternity, admired and feared among the people. They were a power to be reckoned with both religiously and politically.

The word *Pharisee*—Hebrew, *Parush*—means a separated one. They separated themselves for greater holiness and in order to avoid defilement by the unlearned and the illiterate, who did not know or observe strictly the laws pertaining to ritual purity. Their striking appearance distinguished the Pharisees from the common people, called *am ha-aretz*—the people of the land, the rustics or ignoramuses.

The Pharisees usually wore white outer garments, fastened with fine silk girdles and bordered with fringes (*tsitsit*), which some liked to enlarge and make conspicuous (Mt. 23:5). They wore phylacteries on their foreheads and left arms, basing this on a literal interpretation of Exodus 13:9: "And it shall be for a sign unto thee upon thine hand, and for a memorial between thine eyes, that the LORD's law may be in thy mouth: for with a strong hand hath the LORD brought thee out of Egypt."

The phylacteries or *tefilin*, the square "prayer boxes" worn on the forehead and left arm during prayer, were not in universal use among the Jews at that time. The Pharisees, however, wore them as a distinguishing mark of their piety, and apparently attributed to them magical powers.[7]

These phylacteries were considered more sacred than the golden plate on the forehead of the high priest, since its inscription contained only once the name of Jehovah, while the phylacteries had the name of Jehovah 23 times. The Pharisees maintained that Jehovah Himself wears phylacteries and studies the Torah.[8]

The Pharisees, whose beginnings go back to the early part of the second century BC, were a profoundly religious, highly nationalistic, and patriotic element among Jewry. They violently opposed all attempts at Hellenization or assimilation of the Jews. At first they supported the Maccabean revolt against the Syrians (around 165 BC). However when, in due course, the descendants of the Maccabees became worldly-minded, usurping for themselves the crown of David in addition to the high priestly mitre, the Pharisees turned away from them. The Hasmonean dynasty was finally replaced by the half-Jewish, half-Idumean (Edomite) dynasty inaugurated by Herod, so-called the Great, who married the princess Mariamne, the last descendant of the Hasmonean dynasty.

In an age when the priestly hierarchy, due to its worldliness and greed, was greatly discredited in the eyes of the common people, it was natural that the Pharisees, who exhibited unusual piety and were opposed to Grecian ways and alien morals, should be popular and highly respected. According to Josephus,[9] the fraternity of Pharisees was a mere 6,000. Yet this small group has molded and shaped the religious thinking of the Jews for the last 2,000 years. They were the ones who gave Judaism its historical character and direction. To be a Pharisee was to belong to a proud and greatly honored company of men, so that Paul could boast of being a Pharisee of the Pharisees (Acts 23:6). In the eyes of the Jews this was a far greater honor than being a Roman citizen.

The antecedents of the Pharisaic movement can be traced back to the times of Ezra the Scribe. In his day there was a great religious revival when the people separated themselves (*Nivdalim*) from the filthiness of the heathen (Ezra 6:21; 9:1; 10:2; Neh. 9:2).

Entering into a solemn league or covenant, these early covenanters called themselves *Hasidim,* the pious ones, or saints. They were the ones who set themselves against the paganizing influences of the Hellenist cities which sprang up in and around Palestine (Gaza, Askelon, Sebaste, Caesarea, Tyre, Gadara, Pella, and many others). These Grecianized cities threatened to engulf Palestine in a sea of paganism. In the days of the Maccabees the Hasidim, now called Pharisees, rallied around them, only to desert them later when the Maccabees became a cruel, self-seeking, and worldly little dynasty.

The Pharisees were organized in a strict fraternity with different ranks. The ordinary Pharisee or *Haver* ("comrade" in Hebrew) only bound himself to Levitical purity and to the strict interpretation of the laws of tithing (Mt. 23:4).

The higher degrees took stricter orders. A Pharisee was forbidden to buy or sell anything from a non-Pharisee for fear of ritual defilement. The garments of a non-Pharisee defiled a Pharisee, and the garments of a Pharisee of lower rank defiled a Pharisee of a higher rank.[10] In certain respects they resembled the caste system in India, with the Pharisees being the highest caste, "the Brahmins," while the *am ha-aretz*, the common people, were "the untouchables."

The Sadducees, the traditional opponents of the Pharisees, sneered at them saying, "The Pharisees would by and by subject the sun itself to their purification."[11]

Pharisaism (not unlike modern orthodoxy in Israel), in spite of its paucity in numbers, by its very intensity and earnestness, gave direction and form to the religious thinking of the Jews. Even the Sadducees had to respect and often to submit to their views. The Sadducees were literalists, holding to the simple letter of the law, often making the Law even more stringent than the interpretation of the Pharisees, which tended to be more flexible and viable.

The Sadducees did not believe in the resurrection nor in a world to come, claiming that there was no real proof from the Law for the doctrine of the resurrection.[12]

The origin of the name *Sadducee* is obscure. It probably was derived either from the name of the priest Zadok, or perhaps from the Hebrew word *tsaddikim*—the righteous ones. It may even have been used ironically by their opponents, just as the term Methodist was later attached by others to the followers of John Wesley.

The Sadducees represented mainly the rich and aristocratic party of wealthy priests with vested interests in the political and religious status quo. Being political realists, the Sadducees were for cooperation with the seemingly invincible foreign power, the Romans. The Pharisees were basically anti-Roman, and strongly nationalistic in their sentiments.

At first a religious order, the Pharisees became a quasi-political party, and finally ended up as a theological school of thought. They were never a sect in the strict sense, as they did not separate themselves from the synagogue or from the Temple, but rather from the unobserving, and untutored common people whom they held in contempt.

The statement recorded in the Gospel of John fairly reflects the spirit of the Pharisees: "Then answered the Pharisees, Are ye also deceived? Have any of the rulers or of the Pharisees believed on him? But this people who knoweth not the law are cursed" (7:47–49).

Among the Pharisees were several schools of thought. The most famous of these were the house of Hillel and the house of Shammai. Both of these great Jewish teachers and scholars lived in the latter part of the first century before Christ. Of the two schools of thought Shammai's is generally considered the more strict.

THE HERODIONS were a political group connected with the ruling powers who supported the dynasty of Herod (Mt. 22:16; Mk. 3:6; 12:13). Religiously, they inclined toward the Sadducees.

THE ZEALOTS (Simon the Zealot) were radical patriots who sought the abolition of the Roman rule by force. Religiously they leaned toward the Pharisees. An extreme element among the Zealots were known as *Sicarii* (knifers), from the concealed knives they carried in order to attack surreptitiously their opponents, both Romans and Jews.

In addition to the Pharisees and the Sadducees, Josephus and Philo of Alexandria also mention the Essenes, who combined Pharisaism with mysticism and asceticism.

It is very likely that the desert community of Qumran, about whose views and practices we have learned so much from the Dead Sea Scrolls, were related in their views and practices to the Essenes. These Essenes were separated from the world and observed strictly and most punctiliously the rules of purification. They also nurtured strongly the Messianic hope.[13]

All these movements, in spite of a certain community of ideas and aspirations, were nevertheless, in essential thought and in their general direction, far removed from the origins of the Christian faith.

Amidst all this political, social, and spiritual turmoil there were many in Israel who waited for the consolation and redemption of Israel through a God-anointed Savior, the Messiah. Anna the prophetess, Elisabeth the cousin of Miriam, Zacharias the father of John the Baptist, Miriam the mother of Jesus, Joseph her husband, and the lovable figure of the aged Simeon, the saintly priest, belonged to this deeply spiritual and messianically motivated group of people.

It was to such people as these, the poor in spirit and the meek (*anavim*), that Jesus later promised would possess the Kingdom of heaven and inherit the earth (Mt. 5:3–5).

Woman in Jewish Life

The image of the Hebrew woman comes to life as we read the stories and the scattered references to the women of the Old and New Testaments. As we observe their virtues which are extolled and their occasional shortcomings which are decried, it becomes evident that the dignity and status of the Hebrew woman was far superior to that of any of her sisters in the antique world.

The very story of woman's creation, as related in Genesis, implies her essential dignity and basic equality with man. She was created by God to be man's helpmeet (2:18), "bone of his bone and flesh of his flesh." The Hebrew word *ishah*—woman, which is the counterpart of *ish*—man, implies her essential oneness with man. They are both one flesh, "Therefore shall a man leave his father and his mother, and shall cleave unto his wife: and they shall be one flesh" (2:24).

Far from being held in isolation and separated from public view and life, like many of her contemporary sisters, the Hebrew woman might mingle rather freely with her menfolk at home and in society. She was the guardian spirit of family life and of its purity. Her personal example and piety gave the home a spiritual aura, and set her children's feet on the path of the fear of the Lord, which is the beginning of wisdom (Prov. 9:10).

Even as the three patriarchs Abraham, Isaac, and Jacob were held in great reverence, so were also the Four Mothers—Sarah, Rebekah, Leah, and Rachel. We know from the Scriptures what tremendous influence "these holy women of old" wielded. And, although Sarah called her husband "lord" (Gen. 18:12), yet she herself always remained true to her own name, *Sarah,* which means "princess" or "lady." It is interesting to note that one of the women who ministered to Jesus was called Martha, which in Aramaic means "lady" (Lk. 10:38).

It was Miriam, the sister of Moses, who led the children of Israel in the song of triumph at the Red Sea (Ex. 15). It was the women whose hearts were stirred up in wisdom, who contributed so generously toward the erection of the Tabernacle in the wilderness (35:21–9).

The prophetess Deborah is memorialized as a woman of great valor, the victorious captain of Israel's forces, and revered judge of her people (Jud. 4—5).

When churlish Nabal incurs the just wrath of David, his wife, Abigail, in her wisdom and with her gracious hospitality seeks to avert catastrophe from befalling her unworthy husband (1 Sam. 25).

The book of Ruth presents the idyllic story of a woman's devotion to the God of Israel and to her husband's kinfolk. Lovely Ruth, the Moabitess, attains the dignity of an ancestress of King David and of the future Messiah Jesus (Mt. 1:5). She, with her purity and God-fearing demeanor, in some measure removes the stigma of her incestuous great, great-grandmother, the daughter of Lot.

THE HEBREW ODE TO WOMAN

Nowhere in all the world's literature does one find an ode which pays greater trbute to womanhood than that which is recorded in Proverbs 31:10-31:

> *He who finds a woman of valor (has found) a price far above rubies.*
> *The heart of her husband doth safely trust in her, so that he shall have no need of spoil.*
> *She will do him good and not evil all the days of her life.*
> *She seeketh wool, and flax, and worketh willingly with her hands.*
> *She is like the merchants' ships; she bringeth her food from afar.*
> *She riseth also while it is yet night, and giveth meat to her household, and a portion to her maidens.*
> *She considereth a field, and buyeth it: with the fruit of her hands she planteth a vineyard.*
> *She girdeth her loins with strength, and strengtheneth her arms.*
> *She perceiveth that her merchandise is good: her candle goeth not out by night.*
> *She layeth her hands to the spindle, and her hands hold the distaff.*
> *She stretcheth out her hands to the poor; yea, she reacheth forth her hands to the needy.*

She is not afraid of the snow for her household: for all her household are clothed with scarlet.

She maketh herself coverings of tapestry; her clothing is silk and purple.

Her husband is known in the gates, when he sitteth among the elders of the land.

She maketh fine linen, and selleth it; and delivereth girdles unto the merchant.

Strength and honor are her clothing; and she shall rejoice in time to come.

She openeth her mouth with wisdom; and in her tongue is the law of kindness.

She looketh well to the ways of her household, and eateth not the bread of idleness.

Her children arise up, and call her blessed; her husband also, and he praiseth her.

Many daughters have done virtuously, but thou excellest them all.

Favor is deceitful, and beauty is vain: but a woman that feareth the LORD, she shall be praised.

Give her of the fruit of her hands; and let her own works praise her in the gates.

In the second century BC, apocryphal book, *The Wisdom of Jeshua Ben-Sira*, we find a similar hymn in praise of the good wife:

A good wife—blessed is her husband. The number of his days is doubled.

A worthy wife cherisheth her husband, and he fulfilleth the years of his life in peace.

A good wife is a good portion;

She shall be given as a portion to them that fear the Lord. Whether rich or poor, his heart is cheerful,

And his face is merry at all times.[1]

Ben-Sira, however, was well acquainted with the opposite of "the good wife" and had also much to say about the wickedness of women:

"Any wound, only not a heart-wound! Any wickedness, only not the wickedness of a woman!...I would rather dwell with a lion and a dragon, than keep house with a wicked woman."[2]

The high respect in which the Jewish women were held can be seen in the following statement. Commenting on the creation of woman from Adam's rib, an ancient rabbi declares: "It is as if Adam had exchanged a pot of earth for a precious jewel."[3]

NEW TESTAMENT WOMAN

Decisive for the position of women in the New Testament period was the attitude of Jesus Himself to womanhood. How understanding, gentle, and compassionate this relationship was. Yet it never degenerated into sentimentality or mawkishness.

In contrast to the pious folks of His day, who avoided any contact with women, Jesus never shunned them.

Near the city of Sychar, He offered a woman (a Samaritan woman, at that) the water of life in exchange for a draft of cool water from Jacob's well (Jn. 4:6–39). He hearkened to the agonized plea of a Syrophenician woman on behalf of her child and praised her faith (Mt. 15:28). He breathed new life into the body of a little girl with the tender, unforgettable words, *Talitha cumi*—Little girl arise (Mk. 5:41). He defended the woman caught in adultery against the harsh justice which the self-righteous of His generation would have meted out to her (Jn. 8:1–11).

In stark contrast to the mores of His time, Jesus often enjoyed the hospitality of Martha and Mary's home and conversed with them about His Kingdom (Lk. 10:38–42). Women ministered to Him with their substance (8:2–3). He exorcized the demons which possessed poor Mary Magdalene, and transformed her blighted life into a new, radiant personality (v. 2).

Is it any wonder that some whom He helped wept at His feet and wiped them with their hair (7:36–38), while others anointed Him with their most precious ointment in preparation for His death (Jn. 12:1–8)?

The relationship of our Lord and His disciples to womanhood was truly ennobling and uplifting. It was entirely out of keeping with the spirit of the times.

Appropriately, the birth of Jesus was hymned by His mother, Miriam, by Anna the prophetess, and glorified by Elisabeth. Heartbroken women mourned His death at the cross. The first glimpse of His resurrected body was vouchsafed to a devout woman, Mary Magdalene (Miriam of the village of Magdala, Jn. 20:11–18).

C. G. Montefiore, the well-known Jewish scholar of liberal Judaism, freely concedes that Jesus was "the great champion of womanhood":

The attitude of Jesus towards women is very striking. He breaks through oriental limitations in more directions than one. For (1) he associates with, and is much looked after by, women in a manner which was unusual; (2) he is more strict about divorce; (3) he is also more merciful and compassionate. He is a great champion of womanhood. ...If he had done no more than this, he might justly be regarded as one of the great teachers of the world.[4]

And again, "the relations of Jesus towards women, and of theirs towards him seem to strike a new note, and a higher note, and to be off the line of Rabbinic tradition."[5]

Jesus Himself set the supreme example that in Christ there is neither Greek nor barbarian, bond or free, male or female, but all are one in Him (Gal. 3:28).

In the New Testament we meet with a representative group of noble women, such as Dorcas, who was given to charity and to the making of garments for the poor (Acts 9:36–39). She apparently was the first president of the original ladies' auxiliary. Lydia, the capable business woman, was the first female convert to Christ in Europe; women like Lois, Eunice, Phoebe, and Priscilla, who were brought up under the sound of Jehovah's Word, towered high above the women of the classic world, even when they were at their best. It is enough to read the works of Homer and Plato, or of the Greek tragedians and historians, or the works of such Roman classic writers as Horace, Ovid, or Cicero to realize how vastly superior was the moral tone and the spiritual atmosphere which exalted the Jewish woman above her contemporaries.

By way of contrast we hear, for instance, that in Sparta extra marital relations were sanctioned by society if likely to produce healthy offspring.[6]

In the Greek world, woman was generally considered to be so inferior to man that he recognized in her no other end than to minister to his pleasure or to become the mother of his children.[7]

Thucydides, in his famous funeral oration, puts these words in the mouth of Pericles,

If I am to speak of womanly virtues to those of you who will hence-
forth be widows, let me sum them up in one short admonition: To
a woman not to show more weakness than is natural to her sex is a
great glory and not to be talked about for good or evil among men. [8]

Or again, "A woman is necessarily an evil, and he is a lucky man who catches her in the mildest form," says one of Thucydides' characters in *Menander.* [9]

The great orator Demosthenes maintained that every man requires beside his wife two mistresses. [10]

Euripides, a fifth-century contemporary of Nehemiah and Ezra, in his tragedy Hippolytus, puts the following words of counsel into the mouth of a trusted family servant who is trying to persuade her lovelorn mistress to commit incest with her stepson:

How many men of sterling character, when they see their wives
unfaithful, pretend as though they saw it not. How many fathers,
when their sons have gone astray, assist them in their love affairs?
It is part of human wisdom to conceal the shameful deed. Nor
should men aim at too great refinement in life. It is nothing but
pride to wish to rival gods in perfection.

Granted that this sordid advice does not represent Greek morality at its best. Nevertheless it does reflect the popular morals of the times among the Greeks.

How far removed this is from the biblical injunction: "Ye shall be holy, for I am holy" (Lev. 11:44).

There was a deep gap between Jewish and Greek ideas of woman's position. Biblical womanhood and family morals tower high above even the best which Greek philosophy and ideals had to offer. Even such great philosophers as Socrates and Plato, in the famous treatise "Symposium," extol homosexualism and similar perverse practices as examples of "pure love."

Roman writers give us a rather dismal picture of moral or, rather, amoral conditions which prevailed in Rome during the first century BC, and during the following centuries.

Toward the end of the first century AD, the satirist Juvenal, admittedly quite a misogynist, in his ballad of "Bad Women" thus portrayed the Roman ladies of his day: "Women's lust is the least of their sins. Now-a-day a woman eats great oysters at midnight and drinks till the roof spins round. My old friends advise, keep your women at home, under lock and key. Yes, and who will guard the guards?"[11]

As for conditions among the so-called barbarians, no comparison can be made between their women's social position and that of Jewish womanhood. To quote just one example, Julius Caesar, in his *Wars*, book 6, chapter 2, speaking about the customs of the Gauls with whom he was at war in the middle of the first century BC, observes:

Husbands have power of life and death over their wives as well as over their children. When the head of any noble family dies, his relatives meet together, and if there is anything suspicious about the way he died, they examine his wives under torture, as we do in the case of slaves; if guilt is proved, the punishment is a slow and very painful death.

As late as the second century, the Church Father Clement of Alexandria, in his treatise "The Instructor," thus bewailed the manners and morals of contemporary women:

At the dawn of day, mangling, and plastering themselves over with certain compositions, they chill the skin, furrow the flesh with poisons, and with curiously prepared washes, thus blighting their own beauty....And these women are carried about over the temples, sacrificing and practising divination day by day, spending their time with fortune-tellers, and begging priests, and disreputable old women; and they keep up old wives' whisperings over their cups, learning charms and incantations from soothsayers, to the ruin of the nuptial bonds.[12]

All in all, in spite of occasional lapses and moral declines scathingly denounced in Isaiah 3:16–24, the moral tone of family life among the Jews and the position of their women was unequalled among the nations of the antique world, civilized or barbarian.

Only a God-inspired ethos could be the origin of Israel's exalted idea of womanhood and family life. Herein was one of the peculiar attractions which Jewish life and faith exercised upon their neighbors, and often filled their synagogues with Gentile *seboumenoi*—fearers of God.

WOMAN IN THE TALMUD

The attitude of the ancient rabbis toward women was far from uniform. While there were instances of high regard for womanhood, yet, on the whole, the position of Jewish woman under rabbinical law, probably due to social customs prevailing among neighboring peoples, deteriorated to some extent. In the ancient Hebrew prayer book the Orthodox Jew still continues even today to thank God that He has not created him "a goy, a slave, or a woman."[13]

Woman's glory became a reflected glory from that of her husband and sons: "Wherewith do women acquire merit? By sending their children to learn Torah in the synagogue and their husbands to study in the school of the Rabbis."[14]

Some rabbis attributed to her serious faults, saying that women are gluttonous, eavesdroppers, lazy, and jealous, also querulous and garrulous.[15]

Elsewhere it was said, "Ten measures of speech descended to the world; women took nine and men one."[16]

Conversation with a woman, even greeting her in the street, was to be avoided as much as possible because that leads to sin. This is why the disciples were so surprised to find Jesus conversing privately not only with a Samaritan, but with a woman at that (Jn. 4:27).

In Jewish tradition woman might aspire to be a footstool for her husband in paradise, but not to be his equal in the blessed home of the departed.

THE JEWISH HOME

The difference between Jew and Gentile was not only religious but social. Even the appearance of a Jewish town or village was different from a pagan settlement. Many of the towns of Palestine had walls surrounded by moats. The city was entered through massive gates covered with iron and locked by bars and bolts. Within the gate the elders sat, discussing public affairs and settling disputes. From the gates a visitor would continue into the public square where the country people brought their farm produce for sale, and the merchants would clamorously extol the fine qualities of their goods, some of which were imported from foreign lands. In the narrow street (*shuk*) the tradesmen had their stores or stands where they sold their manufactures: sandals and clothing, household furnishings and a great variety of fruit, vegetables, and fish. Modern Nazareth has preserved a typical example of such an ancient *shuk* or market street.

Somewhere in a corner of the market there would be heard the voice of a learned rabbi teaching his disciples the traditions of the elders. In the night every home would kindle a light which would stay lighted all night, shining into the street.

A Jewish town or city was a well organized municipality with city police, sanitation, drainage, public baths, and public schools. Safety measures to prevent diseases and epidemics were strictly enforced. Weights, measures, and prices of foodstuffs were subject to official inspection.[17]

The home was entered by a door, furnished with a knocker, which led into an inner court. "Behold, I stand at the door and knock" (Rev. 3:20). From the court one would reach the family living quarters, the dining hall, the sleeping quarters, etc. The furniture consisted of tables, couches, chairs, lamps. Hospitality was considered a godly custom. Circumcisions, weddings, holy days, and festive observances were special occasions for conviviality. Abraham was extolled as a high example of hospitality in the Old and New Testaments as well as in later rabbinical tradition (Gen. 18; Heb. 13:2).

CHAPTER FOUR

Marriage and Family Life

Marriage and the rearing of a family were considered among the Jews a sacred duty in accordance with God's first commandment to Adam and Eve. "And God blessed them, and God said unto them, Be fruitful, and multiply and replenish the earth, and subdue it" (Gen. 1:28).

According to the Mishnah (the earliest part of the Talmud containing a collection of legal traditions explaining the laws of Moses or derivable from the principles of these laws, finally compiled by R. Judah the Prince at the close of the second century AD), a wife could be acquired by three means: By money, by a marriage contract known as a *ketubah,* or by cohabitation. The latter did not have to be in the literal sense, but under certain conditions might be assumed to have taken place if the woman was alone with a man.[1]

A young man between 16 and 22 was considered of marriageable age as the saying went, "A young man of 18 for the canopy." A girl was considered of age when 12 years and one day old. In the Talmud, betrothal was called *erusin,* and marriage *kiddushin*—sanctification, because "the husband prohibits his wife to the whole world like an object which is sanctified to the sanctuary."[2] This attitude toward marriage implied chastity in both parties. Polygamy, though sanctioned, was frowned upon.[3]

Betrothal or espousals in ancient Israel was much more than an engagement in our times, and was practically equivalent to a formal marriage.

The engaged bride was legally considered as a wife.[4] If her bridegroom died before they came together she was considered a widow in every respect and was subject to a levirate marriage,[5] in accordance with the law of the childless widow (Dt. 25:5–10). A betrothal could only be broken by a regular divorce.

This fact must be remembered if we are to understand the marital status of Miriam and Joseph. The laws concerning betrothal and marriage are discussed in great detail in the Mishnah, in the Tractates Kiddushin (Sanctification) and Ketuboth (Marriage Contracts).

However, many of the laws and practices described in the Mishnah probably pertain to a later time than those which prevailed at the turn of the era.

In ancient times, the bride was purchased by the prospective bridegroom for a sum of money or for services rendered. This took place in the case of Jacob, as described in Genesis 29. The marriage was arranged between the parents of the young man and the young woman, or between their representatives.

However, the consent of the bride-to-be was required.

From the moment of her betrothal until she married, the espoused bride remained in the home of her parents, and could not be betrothed to another man, just as if she were already married. In two Scripture passages "the betrothed woman" is designated as "wife" (2 Sam. 3:14; Dt. 22:23–24).

At the betrothal a sum of money was paid by the bridegroom (*mohar*) to the prospective father-in-law, the minimum of which was, for a virgin, 200 *zuzim*; for a widow half the amount. The price went up considerably with the wealth and social position of the bride and bridegroom, and could be as high as 1 million *dinars* as in the case of the famous Nicodemus of John 3, who is called Nakdimon in the Talmud. In case of divorce the bride kept the money.

The value of the silver dinar (Latin, *denarius*), called in the Talmud *zuz,* was about 16-17 cents. Its actual purchasing power is hard to establish. In the times of Christ it was the daily wages of a laborer (Mt. 20:2). It must have had the purchasing power of at least $3 and probably more.[6]

In addition, lavish gifts were made by the bridegroom or his representatives to the bride's parents and family. A classic example of this custom is recorded in Genesis 24.

It is interesting to note that the custom of *mohar,* paying for the bride, is still practiced among the oriental Jews today.[7]

In later times the money was given to the prospective bride herself. In addition, the parents of the bride would give her a dowry of 50 *zuzim*.

The bride's parents were obliged to provide her with a trousseau, that is, with suitable clothing and household goods. A rich bride would also get a number of servants. In addition the bridegroom would receive from her parents a gift of cash, which he could use to establish himself in business. This was known as *Nadan*. This custom is still common among some Jewish people even today.

The bridegroom was also obligated to provide his wife with a home and a suitable household and with means of sustenance, according to her station in life.

After all arrangements were made, at the appointed time the families of the bride and bridegroom met in the presence of witnesses. The groom gave the bride a ring, and promised to observe the terms of the contract. Then he would give the bride a symbolic token, usually a small coin or some other object of value.

After the contract was signed, the guests began to make merry. From then on, their status was that of a married couple, although as a rule they would not live together. A proper marriage ceremony would follow in about a year's time in the case of a virgin, or at least 30 days in the case of a widow. However, the couple could come together and live as man and wife, and their children would be considered as legitimate, although such mode of wedding was frowned upon by society.

On the wedding day the bride bathed (Judith 10:3), put on richly embroidered white robes (Ps. 45:13–14), decked herself with jewels, put the bridal girdle around her waist and covered herself with a veil (Gen. 24:65). The bridegroom, dressed handsomely with a garland on his head, went forth to the home of his bride in the company of musicians, singers, torchbearers, or lampbearers (1 Macc. 9:39; Mt. 25:7). After receiving the bride from her parents, with their blessing, he returned to his own home or his parents' with music and dancing (Ps. 45:15; Song 3:6–11). A feast was served at the house of the groom (Jn. 2:1,9). For the first time the groom was permitted to associate with his bride. Later the bride was escorted to the nuptial chamber by her parents (Gen. 29:23), while the groom was escorted by his companion or "the friend of the bridegroom" (Jn. 3:29).

In later times, the betrothal and marriage were merged into one ceremony.

The form of betrothal pronounced by the bridegroom was this: "Be thou betrothed unto me with this ring (or object) in accordance with the laws of Moses and Israel." From this point on the young woman was the espoused wife, as in the case of Miriam and Joseph. A separate wedding ceremony was not essential, and is not mentioned in the Gospels. However, still later, an additional wedding ceremony after the espousals became an essential part of the marriage procedure. Virgins usually were married on Wednesdays, widows on Thursdays. (The courts sat on Thursdays, and a bridegroom could complain to the court if the occasion warranted.)

The present manner of performing a wedding ceremony is this: The bride and groom stand under the canopy. The wedding ceremony is usually performed by a rabbi, who fills a cup of wine and pronounces the following benediction: "Blessed art thou, O Lord our God, King of the universe, who createst the fruit of the vine."

Then he continues:

> Blessed art thou, O Lord our God, King of the universe, who has sanctified us by thy commandments, and hast given us command concerning forbidden marriages; who hast disallowed unto us those that are betrothed, but hast sanctioned unto us such as are wedded to us by the rite of the canopy and the sacred covenant of wedlock. Blessed art thou, O Lord, who sanctifiest thy people Israel by the canopy and sacred covenant of wedlock.

At this point, the bridegroom places the ring upon the forefinger of the right hand of the bride, and says:

"Behold, thou art consecrated unto me by this ring, according to the Law of Moses and of Israel."[8]

DIVORCE

Since the purpose of marriage was the rearing of a family, sterility was considered sufficient cause for divorce. The husband was even obliged to divorce a barren wife after 10 years of childless marriage.[9] Adultery was also grounds for divorce as in Matthew 19:9: "And I say unto you, whosoever shall put away his wife, except it be for fornication and shall marry another, committeth adultery: and whoso marrieth her which is put away doth commit adultery."

These words of our Savior were in protest to rabbinical law which permitted divorce even for trivial reasons, such as "speaking to a man without witnesses, giving her husband untithed food, speaking loudly in her home so that neighbors could hear her voice, or cursing her in-laws."[10]

The biblical injunction of Deuteronomy 24:1 concerning divorce was interpreted very broadly. The famous Hillel maintained that a man might divorce his wife if she spoiled a dish for him, or even if he found a woman who pleased him more.

Nevertheless, though permitting divorce in theory, in practice the rabbis discouraged divorce. A rabbinical saying had it that heaven weeps when a husband divorces his wife. Polygamy was allowed but not encouraged. The domestic duties which a wife had to perform for her husband were clearly stipulated.

These are works which the wife must perform for her husband: grinding flour and baking bread and washing clothes and cooking food and giving suck to her child and making ready his bed and working in wool. If she brought him in one bondwoman she need not grind or bake or wash; if two, she need not cook or give her child suck; if three, she need not make ready his bed or work in wool; if four, she may sit (all the day) in a chair.

R. Eliezer says: "Even if she brought him a hundred bondwomen he should compel her to work in wool, for idleness leads to unchastity."[11]

Although, under rabbinical law, the position of the woman was not as favorable as in the former centuries, yet, generally speaking, the moral tone of Jewish family life was far superior to that of any of the peoples of the ancient world. In fact, outside of the Jewish community, it was hardly possible to speak of family life in the real sense of the word. This is why the moral standards of Judaism presented such an attraction to the dissolute Hellenist and Roman world, and won for itself many proselytes among the Gentiles, as evidenced in the New Testament and later in the Talmud.

CHILDREN

Children, especially sons, were considered a gift from God. The rabbis expressed this idea through a play of words: "Sons" (in Hebrew *banim*) are "builders" (*bonim*), because they build the future of the family and of the community. [12]

The relationship of children to parents was anchored to the fifth commandment, "Honor thy father and mother." This commandment was given the broadest interpretation to include all social, moral, and economic aspects of life. According to the rabbis a son was bound, if necessary, to beg for his father in order to provide his needs. Children became independent of parental tutelage only after marriage or when able to earn a living. On the other hand, fathers were obliged to provide for their minor children, to educate them, and to teach them a trade. Aged persons were to be respected as if they were pieces of the broken tables of the Law. [13]

Something of the importance of children in the life of the biblical family can be gleaned from the number of terms used to describe children in their various stages of growth and development:

ben—son
bath—daughter
yeled—babe
yonek—suckling
olal—older suckling
gamul—weaned one
taph—skirt clinger
alma—young maiden, virgin
elem—young man
naar—boy
naarah—girl (12 years and older)
bachur—young fellow-warrior

The family has always played an all-important role in the life of the Jewish people. Israel as a people in itself was an extension of the family, of the clan or the tribe.

Among the Jews childlessness was considered a disaster. "A childless person is accounted as dead." [14]

While sons were considered a great blessing and a mark of God's favor, daughters were looked upon as a minor blessing.

"Lo, sons (children) are a heritage of the LORD: and the fruit of the womb is his reward. As arrows are in the hand of a mighty man; so are sons (children) of the youth" (Ps. 127:3–4). (The King James Version translates the word "sons" not quite correctly as "children.")

In Numbers Rabbah 9:5, the talmudical commentary on the book of Numbers, the priestly benediction is explained thus: "The LORD bless thee and keep thee." This means: "Bless thee with sons, and keep thee from daughters."

EDUCATION OF CHILDREN

The education and training of children was inculcated in the Old Testament as a primary duty of parents:

And these words, which I command thee this day, shall be in thine heart, and thou shalt teach them diligently unto thy children, and shalt talk of them when thou sittest in thine house, and when thou walkest by the way, and when thou liest down, and when thou risest up (Dt. 6:6–7).

The rabbis emphasized the same thought :

"He who rears his children in the Law (or Torah) is among those who enjoy the fruit in this world while the capital remains for him in the world to come."[15]

"Whoever has a son laboring in the Torah is as though he never dies."[16]

As a result of this keen desire to educate their children, the Jews were the first to develop a universal and compulsory school system, which was probably in existence already in the first century BC.[17] Very likely the boy Jesus attended such a religious school in His home town, Nazareth.

It is interesting to note that the apocryphal nativity Gospels have a number of legends depicting Jesus as a schoolboy. Little children first learned about God and biblical heroes at the feet of their mothers and grandmothers.

"I call to remembrance the unfeigned faith that is in thee, which dwelt first in thy grandmother Lois, and thy mother Eunice; and I am persuaded that in thee also" (2 Tim. 1:5).

Their schooling usually began at the age of six or even at five.[18]

Teachers were held in highest esteem. Sometimes they were even given preference over parents. "For parents bring children into the world, whereas teachers bring them to the life of the world to come."[19]

METHOD OF INSTRUCTION

The chief method of instruction was repetition and memorization. The words, "Thou shalt teach them diligently" (Dt 6:7) literally mean "Thou shalt repeat," or "Thou shalt keep on repeating."

"If a student learn Torah and does not repeat it again and again, he is like a man who sows but does not reap."[20]

"He who repeats his lesson a hundred times is inferior to him who repeats it one hundred and one times."[21]

The chief aim of the elementary school was to instruct in Hebrew and in the Torah. Instruction usually began with the book of Leviticus. The reasoning behind it was this: "Since the children are pure and the sacrifices are pure, let the pure come and occupy themselves with pure things."[22]

At the age of 10 the boy advanced to the learning of "the traditions of the Elders." Those who were considered exceptionally gifted continued in a rabbinical academy. This made it possible for a man eventually to become a scribe (*sofer*)—a learned scholar of the Law comparable to a doctor of theology—so frequently mentioned in the New Testament. Incidentally, the scribes were the intellectual elite among the Pharisees.

The learning of Greek and worldly wisdom was generally frowned upon. One rabbi declared: "Cursed be the man who has his son taught Greek philosophy."[23]

EDUCATION OF WOMEN DISCOURAGED

However, girls were not encouraged to study the Torah: "Whoever teaches his daughter Torah is as though he taught her obscenity."[24]

Another rabbi asserted: "Let the words of the Torah rather be destroyed by fire than imparted to women."[25]

This attitude was probably motivated by the fear that women students would come in closer touch with men, which might lead to laxity in morals. Overpious women were also decried: "The female Pharisee" was called "a destroyer of the world."[26]

The domain of the Jewish woman was the home, and her chief task was looking after her husband and raising her children during their tender age. She had the responsibility of seeing to it that her home was a godly place. Although not admitted to public life or to active participation in public worship, she was permitted to attend the synagogue services, and was the guardian of the lofty moral and spiritual standards of family life. It was considered a great merit for a woman to take all burdens from her husband and sons, so that they might give themselves to the study of the Law and the traditions of the Elders. Consequently, Jewish women were quite often the breadwinners and the actual heads of their families, while their husbands became students and celebrated scholars of the Torah.

The famous rabbi Akiba, who died during Bar Kochba's revolt against Rome (AD 135) was for many years supported by his ambitious wife, Rachel, until the erstwhile shepherd boy became one of the most illustrious luminaries of Judaism.

As a result of these social and religious conditions, the devotions and piety of Jewish women were of a very simple and heartfelt nature, often strikingly beautiful in their humble faith and great warmth and reliance upon God. It was among certain of these women, before and during the time of Christ, that the Messianic hope was most fervently cherished and nurtured (Lk. 2:38).

No doubt Miriam, brought up in the simplicity of rural life and sharing the faith, the traditions, and the hopes of her people, belonged to the circle of women who waited fervently for the salvation of Israel.

PART TWO

Miriam in the Gospels

CHAPTER FIVE

New Testament References to Miriam

Here is a list of all New Testament passages in which the mother of Jesus is directly or indirectly referred to. It will be noticed that the Gospel of Luke provides us with the most information on the subject.

It seems that Luke the evangelist made it his business to set forth in orderly fashion "those things which are most surely believed among us" (1:1). With this purpose in view he carefully gathered and sifted the information obtained from those who were eyewitnesses of the events described in his Gospel. It is possible he may have had access to persons closely connected with the early life of Jesus or with members of His immediate family. He may have even known Miriam herself and secured from her information unknown to the other evangelists.

Seeking to portray Jesus as the Son of Man, Luke emphasized incidents connected with the nativity and early life of Jesus.

Joseph, the husband of Miriam, Matthew 1:16
The annunciation, Luke 1:26–38
Miriam visits Elisabeth, Luke 1:39–45
The Magnificat, Luke 1:46–56
Joseph and Miriam, Matthew 1:18–25
The birth of Jesus, Luke 2:1–7
The shepherds' adoration, Luke 2:16–20
The purification of Miriam, Luke 2:21–24
Simeon's blessing, Luke 2:33–35
The wise men, Matthew 2:11
Flight into Egypt, Matthew 2:13–14
The boy Jesus in the Temple, Luke 2:41–52
The marriage feast in Cana, John 2:1–12

"Who is my mother?," Matthew 12:46–50; Mark 3:31–35
"Is not his mother called Mary?," Matthew 13:54–55; Mark 6:2–3;
John 6:42
His brethren and His sisters, Matthew 13:55–58; Mark 6:3; John 6:42
Miriam at the cross, John 19:25–27
Miriam in the upper room, Acts 1:12–14

This is the very modest amount of information about Miriam and her immediate family contained in the New Testament. It is quite insufficient to reconstruct the life of the mother of our Lord.

From this extreme meagerness of data one can hardly avoid gaining the impression that here we have a deliberate design to prevent the forming of a personal cult of the virgin mother, so alien and repugnant to the Hebrew mind, and to direct instead the reader of the New Testament to Miriam's son, Yeshua the Messiah, the bearer of redemption. Nevertheless, a careful analysis of the above New Testament references to Miriam in addition to the well-known historical and religious background of that period should provide us with some helpful insights into her singular life. Before going further, we shall first consider briefly the person of Joseph, the husband of Miriam and guardian of Jesus during the perilous years of His infancy and tender age.

JOSEPH, THE HUSBAND OF MARY

"And Jacob begat Joseph the husband of Mary, of whom was born Jesus, who is called Christ" (Mt. 1:16).

With these words we are introduced, for the first time in the New Testament, to Miriam and to her husband, Joseph. If we know little about the mother of Jesus, we know even less about Joseph. The Gospel references to him are exceedingly meager. We only know he was of the tribe of Judah and of the house of David (vv. 1,2), a carpenter by trade (13:55). He apparently taught his foster son, Jesus, the same trade (Mk. 6:3). This was entirely in keeping with Jewish custom, which enjoined fathers to teach their children a trade. Oftentimes a particular trade or occupation was in a family for many generations.

Bar Kappara said, "Let a man always teach his son a clean and easy handicraft." "What is such?" "R. Judah said, "Embroidery."

Rabbi said, "There is no handicraft which can disappear from the world. Happy is he whom his parents see engaged in a respected handicraft; the world cannot exist without druggists, or tanners; happy is he whose handicraft is that of a druggist, and woe to him whose handicraft is that of a tanner." (Tanning was considered one of the most loathsome occupations and was usually conducted on the edge or outside the city. The example of Simon the tanner's house in Joppa, "whose house was by the seaside" was rather typical (Acts 10:6.)

Apparently, Joseph was a devout man of simple faith and of a gentle nature (Mt. 1:19), obedient and submissive to the will of God (v. 24).

He was a humble, hardworking man whom God saw fit to choose as the husband and protector of Miriam and of her miracle child, Jesus.

It is interesting to note that not a single word of Joseph's is recorded in the Gospels. He seems to fade into the background. In the divine drama of salvation no one, not even Miriam or Joseph, highly favored as they were, must "steal the play" from the Author of salvation, Christ Himself.

The last time Joseph is referred to indirectly is on the occasion of the family's pilgrimage from Nazareth to the Temple in Jerusalem (Lk. 2:43), when the boy Jesus became separated from His parents for some time. At that time Joseph shared with Miriam the natural anxiety of distraught parents over the disappearance of their beloved child. After this, every reference or allusion to Joseph ceases. The statement of John 6:42, "And they said, Is not this Jesus, the son of Joseph, whose father and mother we know? How is it then that he saith, I came down from heaven?" does not cast light on the question whether Joseph was at the time still alive.

When Jesus emerges again as a popular teacher and worker of miracles, some 18 years have passed since His memorable appearance in the Temple. Miriam is alive and so are His brothers and sisters (Mk. 6:3), but Joseph is conspicuous by his absence. Except for the non-committal reference in John 6:42, he is never mentioned again.

Beneath the cross on Calvary Miriam stood alone in her grief. Joseph was not there to comfort her or to take her home. This task was committed by the Man on the cross to the beloved disciple John

(19:25-27). This leads us to assume that sometime during these intervening 18 years Joseph had passed away.

Perhaps, judging by modern standards, Joseph died comparatively young. We must remember however that the average life span in the Roman Empire during that period was about 27 to 30 years, but probably considerably longer for the abstemious and hard-working people of Galilee.

If we assume that Joseph married at the age of 18 to 20, as was the custom among the Jews, and taking under consideration the events in the life of Joseph to which we have alluded above, we can assume that Joseph probably died somewhere between the ages of 40 and 50.

JOSEPH IN THE APOCRYPHA

The very paucity of data concerning Joseph and the later popular beliefs concerning Miriam have encouraged the growth of legends which have come down to us in the various apocryphal or spurious Infancy Gospels. Of these there is a considerable number.

According to these spurious gospels, Joseph was a widower whose wife died young and left him with a family of four boys and two girls. The names of the boys are similar to those mentioned in Matthew 13:55—James, Joses, Simon, and Judas. In addition to these names, the apocryphal fourth-century *History of Joseph the Carpenter* mentions the names of the daughters as Lysia and Lydia.[2] We are told that out of reverence for Miriam Joseph never lived with her as husband and wife. These legends are an obvious effort to explain away the Gospel references to "the brethren and sisters of Jesus" (Mk. 6:3).

The mass of legendary material concerning the immediate family of Jesus must be handled with the greatest of caution. The Church of Rome never accepted these so-called Gospels as authentic, nevertheless it adopted some of their legends as reliable tradition. To give the reader an idea of the kind of legends which were current at that time, we quote from the Book of James, also known as the Protevangelium (second century) :

> *And Mary was in the temple of the Lord as a dove that is nurtured: and she received food from the hand of an angel.*

And when she was twelve years old, there was a council of the priests, saying: Behold Mary is become twelve years old in the temple of the Lord. And they said unto the high priest: Thou standest over the altar of the Lord. Enter in and pray concerning her: And whatsoever the Lord shall reveal to thee, that let us do.

And the high priest took the vestment with the twelve bells and went in unto the Holy of Holies and prayed concerning her. And lo, an angel of the Lord appeared saying unto him; Zacharias, Zacharias, go forth and assemble them that are widowers of the people, and let them bring every man a rod, and to whomsoever the Lord shall show a sign, his wife shall she be. And the heralds went forth over all the country round about Judaea, and the trumpet of the Lord sounded, and all ran thereto.

And Joseph cast down his adze and ran to meet them, and when they were gathered together they went to the high priest and took their rods with them. And he took the rods of them all and went into the temple and prayed. And when he had finished the prayer he took the rods and went forth and gave them back to them: and there was no sign upon them. But Joseph received the last rod: and lo, a dove came forth of the rod and flew upon the head of Joseph. And the priest said unto Joseph: Unto thee hath it fallen to take the virgin of the Lord and keep her for thyself.

And Joseph refused, saying: I have sons, and I am an old man, but she is a girl: lest I became a laughing-stock to the children of Israel. And the priest said unto Joseph: Fear the Lord thy God, and remember what things God did unto Dathan and Abiram and Korah, how the earth clave and they were swallowed up because of their gainsaying. And now fear thou, Joseph, lest it be so in thine house. And Joseph was afraid, and took her to keep her for himself. And Joseph said unto Mary: Lo, I have received thee out of the temple of the Lord: and now do I leave thee in my house, and I go away to build my buildings and I will come again unto thee. The Lord shall watch over thee.[3]

The apocryphal Gospel of Thomas, probably compiled in the fourth
or fifth century AD, preserved many legendary narratives dealing
with the many miraculous events during the infancy and childhood of
Jesus. Some of these legends are repeated in the so-called Gospel of
Pseudo-Matthew. We shall have occasion to refer to these and other
spurious gospels at some later time.

Of special interest to us at this stage is the fourth-century *History
of Joseph the Carpenter*. We are informed that Joseph was 40 years old
when he married, and was married to Mary 49 years and survived her
by one year. This would make him 90 years old when he died.[4]

JOSEPH OF THE HOUSE OF DAVID

The Gospel of Luke 1:27 informs us that Joseph was of the house of
David: "To a virgin espoused to a man whose name was Joseph, of the
house of David; and the virgin's name was Mary."

Since the days of the Hasmonean dynasty (164 BC), the house of
David had come upon evil times. Most of those who could even remotely
be considered as claimants to the throne of David were destroyed by the
Hasmonean rulers and later by those who were of the house of Herod,
famous for its ruthlessness and unprecedented cruelty.

Rome, too, always suspicious of revolt and sedition, sought to remove
all possible claimants to the throne of David.

It is quite possible that at some time in the past the ancestors of
Joseph, aware of their perilous situation, like so many other impoverished
descendants of the house of David, removed themselves from Judea
to Nazareth and settled down to a life of artisans, practicing the trade
of carpentry and ministering to the needs of the small town and its
rustic population, probably helping to build houses, making ploughs
and yokes and household furniture, or utensils. As it was the duty of
a Jewish father to teach his son a trade, Joseph taught his foster son,
Jesus, the craft of a carpenter (Mk. 6:3).

Scattered allusions in the parables of Jesus seem to indicate a famil-
iarity with the carpenter's trade.

JOSEPH "THE TSADDIK"

Joseph must have been an unassuming man, hardworking and of
impeccable character. His dealings with Miriam show a gentleness and

delicacy which indicate a man of high moral character. This is especially discernible from his comportment under the most trying circumstances: "Then Joseph her husband, being a just man, and not willing to make her a public example, was minded to put her away privily" (Mt. 1:19). A "just man"—in Hebrew, *ish tsaddik*—conveys much more than the English translation conveys to the modern man.

We speak of "a perfect gentleman." The Greek ideal of the perfect gentleman was *kalos kai agathos*—beautiful and good, a man whose outward appearance and inward moral values blend into one harmonious personality. The Roman ideal of "the good man" was one who exemplified *Virtus Romana*—Roman valor, a combination of military prowess and civic mindedness.

The Hebrew ideal of "the good man" was *ish tsaddik*, a man who endeavors to live according to the norms of divine righteousness, as revealed in God's law. This is still the Jewish ideal today.

Such a man was Joseph, gentle, considerate, compassionate, with a deep sense of justice, a man who habitually walked in the paths of righteousness and mercy. It was to such a humble and "just man" that God entrusted the child Jesus, the bearer of salvation, and the task of protecting from the suspicions of men His defenseless virgin mother, Miriam.

THE PREDICAMENT OF JOSEPH

Joseph, "being a just man," was certainly caught in a painful predicament: Here was Miriam, "his espoused wife," who "before they came together" as husband and wife "was found with child of the Holy Ghost" (Mt. 1:18). Naturally, he could only assume that his beloved Miriam had become unfaithful to him. What else was he to think? According to the Law of Moses, conjugal unfaithfulness was a capital offense punishable by death through stoning (Lev. 20:10; Jn. 8:5).

But here is where the peculiar nature of Joseph as "a just man" came into evidence. He was unwilling to bring public disgrace or even worse upon his beloved Miriam. So he decided to do what seemed to be the kindest, the most considerate thing under the circumstances: "put her away privily."

Only under the most severe strains of life does the true character of a man come to light. Joseph did not fail. This is why God chose him

for the role of foster parent, and this is why God entrusted to him the
mystery of the supernatural birth of Jesus:

> *But while he thought on these things, behold, the angel of the Lord*
> *appeared unto him in a dream, saying, Joseph, thou son of David,*
> *fear not to take unto thee Mary thy wife: for that which is con-*
> *ceived in her is of the Holy Ghost* (Mt. 1:20).

Writing about this particular event, Edersheim remarks: "Never had
the fortunes of the house of David fallen lower, than when a Herod
sat on its throne, and its lineal representative was a humble village
carpenter, from whose heart doubts of the Virgin-Mother had to be
Divinely chased."[5]

Like Abraham of old, Joseph believed God against all odds. By his
faith, by the tender care with which he surrounded Miriam and the
infant Jesus, by his training of the child in all godliness as well as in
the skill of his craft, Joseph demonstrated that God knew to whom to
entrust a treasure more precious than the human mind could conceive.

CHAPTER SIX

The Annunciation

And in the sixth month the angel Gabriel was sent from God unto a city of Galilee, named Nazareth, to a virgin espoused to a man whose name was Joseph, of the house of David; and the virgin's name was Mary.

And the angel came in unto her, and said, Hail, thou that art highly favored, the Lord is with thee: blessed art thou among women. And when she saw him, she was troubled at his saying, and cast in her mind what manner of salutation this should be. And the angel said unto her, Fear not, Mary: for thou hast found favor with God. And, behold, thou shalt conceive in thy womb, and bring forth a son, and shalt call his name JESUS. He shall be great, and shall be called the Son of the Highest: and the Lord God shall give unto him the throne of his father David: And he shall reign over the house of Jacob for ever; and of his Kingdom there shall be no end.

Then said Mary unto the angel, How shall this be, seeing I know not a man? And the angel answered and said unto her, The Holy Ghost shall come upon thee, and the power of the Highest shall overshadow thee: therefore also that holy thing which shall be born of thee shall be called the Son of God. And, behold, thy cousin Elisabeth, she hath also conceived a son in her old age: and this is the sixth month with her, who was called barren. For with God nothing shall be impossible.

And Mary said, Behold the handmaid of the Lord; be it unto me according to thy word. And the angel departed from her (Lk. 1:26–38).

"IN THE SIXTH MONTH"

With these words the birth of Jesus is brought into an interrelationship with the birth of John the Baptist, in accordance with Old Testament prophecy: "Behold, I will send you Elijah the prophet before the coming of the great and dreadful day of the Lord" (Mal. 4:5).

The same divine power which brought about the birth of John the Baptist was also active at the birth of Jesus, the Redeemer of Israel.

"NAZARETH, A CITY IN GALILEE"

Although Nazareth, like so many other cities in Galilee, is not mentioned in the Old Testament nor in the Talmud, yet it must have been a thriving city at the turn of the era.

Many a scholar and writer has extolled the beauty of the place where Jesus spent his childhood and youth. St. Jerome called Nazareth 'The Flower of Galilee.' In the arcades of its lanes and alley-ways a surprising number of carpenters run their open air workshops and sell their wares. Wooden yokes for oxen, ploughs, and a variety of other implements used by smallholders in the past as well as today are manufactured there.

As in the time of Jesus, women draw water in jars, which they skillfully balance on their heads, from a well at the foot of the hill where a little spring supplies it. 'Ain Maryam,' 'Mary's Well,' has been the name of this fountain from time immemorial. It provides the only water supply for far and near.

Old Nazareth has left many traces behind. It lay farther up the hill than the modern village, and there 1,200 feet above sea level its little houses with their clay walls clustered together, one of them belonging to Joseph the carpenter.

Nazareth, like Jerusalem, is surrounded by hills. But how different is the character of the two scenes, how unlike they are in appearance and atmosphere. There is an air of menace and gloom about the Judaean mountains. They provide a noble and austere background for a world which gave birth to the prophets, these uncompromising

*fighters who pitted their wills against the whole world, who
stormed against wrongs of every sort, against immorality, against
perversions of justice, who pronounced judgment upon the people
and rebuked the nations.*

*Peaceful and charming by contrast are the gentle contours of the
environs of Nazareth. Gardens and fields surround the little
village with its farmers and its craftsmen. Groves of date-palms,
fig trees and pomegranates clothe the encircling hills in friendly
green. The fields are full of wheat and barley, vineyards yield their
delicious fruit and everywhere on the highways and byways grows
an abundance of richly colored flowers.*

*This is the countryside which supplied Jesus with so many of these
lovely parables, the parables of sowing and harvesting, of the wheat
and the tares, and mustard seed, the vineyard and the lilies of the
field.*

*Yet old time Nazareth was not wholly out of touch with the busy
world. The Roman military road from the north which came down
through the hills of Galilee passed Nazareth on its way, and not far
south an ancient caravan route, the busy road for all trade between
Damascus and Egypt, crossed the plain of Jezreel.*[1]

"A VIRGIN ESPOUSED TO A MAN"

The significance of espousals in that particular period of time has been
discussed elsewhere in this study (chapter 4).

THE ANGEL GABRIEL

The name *Gabriel* means "Man of God." Gabriel is mentioned in the
Old Testament where he appeared to Daniel (8:15–16). There his
appearance is described as that of a man, speaking with the voice of a
man. Gabriel's appearance is also described in greater detail in Daniel
10:5–6:

Then I lifted up mine eyes, and looked, and behold a certain man

clothed in linen, whose loins were girded with fine gold of Uphaz:
His body also was like the beryl, and his face as the appearance of
lightning, and his eyes as lamps of fire, and his arms and his feet
like in color to polished brass, and the voice of his words like the
voice of a multitude.

Apparently Gabriel, as God's messenger is sent to announce an
important favor of God. He is so engaged in connection with the birth
of the Redeemer and that of His forerunner John (Lk. 1:11–25).

In Jewish tradition there were four archangels (sometimes seven)
mentioned. Their names were Michael, Gabriel, Uriel, and Raphael. [2]
These angels were always in the presence of God. Michael appears to
be the guardian angel of Israel (Dan. 10:13; Rev. 12:7) and operates in
heaven on behalf of Israel, while Gabriel is God's messenger on Earth.
In Islamic tradition, Gabriel is represented as God's messenger who
revealed the Qur'an to Muhammad.

"AND THE VIRGIN'S NAME WAS MARY"

Mary—in Hebrew, Miriam; in Greek, Mariam or Maria; in Latin,
Maria; in English, Mary. It is perhaps well to bear in mind that if
someone had met Miriam in the streets of Nazareth and called her
"Mary," she would have been surprised to hear herself addressed by
such a foreign-sounding name. This would also have been true of her
son, whose name in Hebrew was *Yeshua.*

The original bearer of the name was Moses' sister, Miriam. The actual
meaning of the name is rather obscure. Some translate the name *Miriam*
"a drop of the sea," others "the fat one." The last may sound strange
and unattractive to modern ears, especially in a land where slimness
is a popular ideal. However, this was not so in antique times. Pleasing
plumpness was a visible sign of prosperity and considered attractive.
Even today, some oriental people seek to fatten up young women of
marriageable age to make them more attractive.

THE TWO MIRIAMS

According to a rabbinical tradition, the name Miriam means "bitterness"
because Moses' sister was born at a time when the Egyptians began
to embitter the lives of the children of Israel by imposing on them

arduous tasks. [3]

Curiously enough, Miriam the sister of Moses is regarded, according to one rabbinical tradition, as a savior of Israel. [4] For her sake a miraculous well, a rock from which water flowed, followed the children of Israel in the wilderness. When Miriam died the well disappeared. [5] Like Moses and Aaron she too died by a kiss from God, and worms did not touch her body. [6]

Thus the original Miriam, the sister of Moses, was subjected to glorifying legends even as the other more famous Miriam, the mother of Jesus, became the subject of deifying myths and legends; only the Jews never made of their legends a dogma which must be believed by all.

Be that as it may, Miriam was apparently a very popular name among the Jews at the turn of the era. No less than six Marys occur in the New Testament. Other biblical names like Joseph and Jacob (James) also occur frequently. The frequency of these names often causes some confusion.

Who was Miriam, who were her parents, what was her background? Unfortunately, the New Testament provides us with scanty facts about the mother of Jesus. However, the New Testament Apocrypha abound with a wealth of traditions and legends which become more and more fantastic the further they were removed in time and in distance from the scene of the New Testament events.

According to the Book of James, one of the apocryphal Infancy Gospels, the parents of Miriam were Joachim and Anna (Hebrew, *Hannah*), who sent her to be raised in the Temple in Jerusalem from the age of three till she was 12 years old—the age of puberty. However, this apparently ancient legend is most unlikely, as there is nothing in contemporary Jewish sources to indicate the practice of bringing up little girls in the Temple.

"THOU ART HIGHLY FAVORED"

"And the angel came in unto her, and said, Hail, thou art highly favored, the Lord is with thee: blessed art thou among women" (Lk. 1:28).

"Highly favored" in Greek, *kecharitomene*, literally, "favored one" or, intensively speaking, "greatly favored." Miriam, in herself, is not the source of favor, as the Latin translation *gratia plena* might imply, but rather, she is the recipient of God's favor, having been chosen to be the mother of heaven's greatest gift to mankind.

"Found favor with God" is a common Old Testament expression which occurs quite frequently (Gen. 18:3, 30:27; Ex. 11:3, 1 Sam. 2:26; Neh. 2:5; Est. 2:15). It means to be looked upon or considered favorably and with benevolence. In the case of Miriam, it was God who was favorably disposed towards her, and not—as some would have it—that she herself is the dispenser of favor.

Franz Delitzsch, in his Hebrew translation of the New Testament, correctly renders the expression "highly favored" with the Hebrew *ki matsath hen*. This is a term often used in the Old Testament and in the later apocryphal writings. "To find favor" is to enjoy the benevolent disposition, or the good will of the one who bestows the favor.

For instance, Joseph found favor in the sight of his keeper (Gen. 39:21). In Exodus 3:21, God promised Moses "I will give this people favor in the sight of the Egyptians."

Jerome, translating the New Testament Greek word *kecharitomene* into Latin, rendered this phrase *gratia plena,* "full of grace." This questionable Latin phrase gave rise to erroneous doctrines which have made the proper understanding of the saintly personality of Miriam more difficult, causing division among Christians.

"THE LORD IS WITH THEE"

Miriam was greatly favored because the Lord was with her in a peculiar way: He was with her in an act of creation, unprecedented and unparalleled since the creation of man. The Lord was with Miriam because hers was the unique privilege to become the mother of the Messiah.

"BLESSED ART THOU AMONG WOMEN"

Miriam, like all faithful daughters of Israel cherished in her heart the great expectation of her people and must have been praying for the coming of the Messiah. Somewhere in the heart of every godly Jewish woman there must have been burning a secret, dim, scarcely uttered hope that she might perhaps be the favored one, and that out of her womb would come forth the Messiah.

Miriam was indeed blessed among women to be chosen of God to be the mother of the Hope of Israel. Hers was the honor of unparalleled distinction, never bestowed upon any other woman. "Blessed art thou among women" was a prophecy exemplified by the sentiments of the women of Jerusalem when they cried: "Blessed...are the paps which thou hast sucked" (Lk. 11:27).

"SHE WAS TROUBLED AT HIS SAYING"

Perhaps "agitated" or "surprised" would be the better rendition of the Greek word *dietarachthe*. She was naturally astonished at the meaning and significance of this peculiar greeting by the angel Gabriel.

"And cast in her mind what manner of salutation this should be" (1:29). These words as well as others (2:51) indicate the reflective and thoughtful nature of Miriam. All that happened to her and to her son Jesus made a deep impression on her mind and her whole being.

"And the angel said unto her, Fear not, Mary, for thou hast found favor with God" (1:30).

On every occasion when the angel Gabriel appears as a messenger of God, he provokes fear in the person to whom he is sent. So it was with Daniel (10:7,12). So it was also in the case of Zacharias (Lk. 1:12–13). And so it was in case of Miriam. The shining appearance of the angel reflecting the majesty of God provoked fear, which might be described as "holy awe," the very essence of reverence.

"And, behold, thou shalt conceive in thy womb and bring forth a son, and shalt call his name JESUS" (1:31).

The supernatural character and virgin birth of the Messiah was, for many centuries, a well-established Messianic belief among the Jews and was never questioned at that period in the religious history of the Jews. Thus we are told in a rabbinic commentary on Isaiah 61:10:

Israel is astounded at His light, and says: Blessed the hour in which the Messiah was created; blessed the womb whence He issued; blessed the generation that sees Him; blessed the eye that is worthy to behold Him; because the opening of His lips is blessing and peace, and His speech quieting of the spirit. Glory and majesty are in His appearance (vesture), and confidence and tranquility in His words; and on His tongue compassion and forgiveness; His prayer is a sweet-smelling odour, and His supplication holiness and purity. Happy Israel, what is reserved for you! Thus it is written: "How manifold is Thy goodness, which Thou hast reserved to them that fear Thee.[7]

Concerning the supernatural birth of the Messiah, we have the following rabbinical opinion: "Rabbi Tanchuma said, in the name of Rabbi Samuel: Eve looked forward to that Seed which is to come from another place. And who is this? This is Messiah the King."[8]

It was much later and as a reaction against Christian teaching that this particular belief, that Messiah was to be born of a virgin, was brought under question and vigorously contested by Jewish teachers.

THE NAME "JESUS"

In the Old Testament names were sometimes much more than labels attached to certain persons. Names often signified the very essence of a person.

In Hebrew, the name Jesus is *Yeshua*. Although not uncommon among the Jews of this period, the name Jesus was peculiarly fitting for the Savior of Israel because, as the Gospel of Matthew explains, "he shall save his people from their sins" (1:21).

Yeshua is an abbreviated form of the name Joshua—"Jehovah is Salvation." It is hardly a coincidence that the name Yeshua is almost identical in sound and spelling with the Hebrew word for salvation, pronounced Yeshuah. *Yeshua*—Jesus, and *Yeshuah*—salvation. Thus, the birth of Jesus and His particular name spell salvation for His people and for all mankind.

Our Lord Himself appears to have been aware of the significance of His name and alluded to it in His memorable meeting with Zaccheus: "And Jesus said unto him, This day is salvation come to this house, forsomuch as he also is a son of Abraham. For the Son of man is come to seek and to save that which was lost" (19:9–10). When Jesus (*Yeshua*) enters a home, then salvation (*Yeshuah*) comes to that home, a play of words discernible only in the Hebrew tongue, but not in any translation of the passage.

"He shall be great, and shall be called the Son of the Highest; and the Lord God shall give unto him the throne of his father David" (1:32).

Jesus was to be the Son of "the most high," a Hebrew designation of God, and at the same time the legitimate heir of the ancestral throne of His father David. Thus, His divine origin and simultaneously His human descent from the line of David are here emphasized. The Messianic nature of His Kingdom is again reaffirmed—a Kingdom without end.

"HOW SHALL THIS BE?"

The surprise expressed by Miriam, "How shall this be, seeing I know not a man?" is natural in her situation. It is not unbelief which prompted her words but a wondering "how?" Disbelief says, "impossible," but faith wonders, "how?"

Sometime ago a friend in Jerusalem, writing to us about a particular problem, ended her letter by saying, "I just wonder how God is going to solve it this time." She was sure that God would do it; she was only wondering how He was going to do it.

"And the angel answered and said unto her, The Holy Ghost shall come upon thee, and the power of the Highest shall over-shadow thee; therefore also that holy thing which shall be born of thee shall be called the Son of God" (1:35).

The angel, by implication, brought to her memory the prophecy of old, of which she, raised in a devout Jewish family in which the promises of God concerning the Messiah were greatly cherished, must have ever been keenly aware.

"Behold, a virgin shall conceive, and bear a son" (Isa. 7:14).

Miriam's was to be the peculiar privilege of making this central Messianic prophecy concerning the manner of Messiah's birth an accomplished reality. The conception by the Holy Spirit was an earnest that the child also would be holy and would be called the Son of God by virtue of the fact that God, through the Holy Spirit, was His Father, as well as by virtue of His matchless, holy life.

The pregnancy of her cousin (in Greek *syngenes*—kinswoman) Elisabeth at an advanced age, after she had been barren all her life, was a further earnest that "with God nothing shall be impossible" (Lk. 1:37).

Here we would like to draw attention to the fact that Elisabeth is expressly designated as *syngenes*, a kinswoman or a cousin, and not "a sister." The significance of this becomes clear when, on another occasion (Mk. 6:2–3), the brothers and sisters of Jesus are mentioned and the Greek words *adelphoi*—brothers, and *adelphai*—sisters are used. It is obvious that the Greeks (and the Hebrews, too) had different words for brothers and sisters and for other relatives. They had no need to use vague or confusing terms which could mean either brother or some other relative, sister or cousin. We shall consider this point in greater detail at a later time.

"For with God nothing shall be impossible" (Lk. 1:37).

In the final analysis, the question of the virgin birth of Christ resolves itself in the question whether we believe in God, what kind of God we believe in, and whether we believe God.

The God of the Scriptures is the God who created the universe *ex nihilo*, and man out of dust (Gen. 2:7). This God caused Abraham and Sarah to give birth to Isaac in spite of their great age, an event which seemed a biological impossibility even to Sarah herself:

> *Therefore Sarah laughed within herself, saying, After I am waxed old shall I have pleasure, my lord being old also? And the Lord said unto Abraham, Wherefore did Sarah laugh, saying, Shall I of a surety bear a child, which am old? Is any thing too hard for the* LORD? (Gen. 18:12–14).

The same God made it possible for Elisabeth to give birth to John the Baptist when she was old. This God could and did, in His sovereign power and will, cause the mother of the Messiah to give birth to Jesus as a virgin, in fulfillment of the ancient prophecy in Isaiah 7:14. "For with God nothing shall be impossible" (Lk. 1:37). The God of the Bible is the God of the impossible. To limit His power is to deny that He is God.

"And Mary said, Behold the handmaid of the Lord; be it unto me according to thy word" (v. 38).

The handmaid of the Lord is another Hebrew expression of self-effacing reverence and humility which we find in the Old Testament. It is used especially by the psalmist, who exclaims "O LORD, truly I am thy servant; I am thy servant, and the son of thine handmaid" (Ps. 116:16). Miriam referred to herself by this term of humble devotion and submission: "Be it unto me according to thy word" (Lk. 1:38).

Roman Catholic theologians attribute to this passage extraordinary importance, basing upon this the teaching which elevates the mother of our Lord to a place of being a partner with God in the work of redemption, the coredemptrix. According to them, the angels in heaven waited, as it were, with bated breath to hear whether Miriam would consent to become the virgin mother of Jesus. "Be it unto me according to thy word." This expression of humble acquiescence to God's will takes on an almost cosmic significance. For, as they reason, if Mary would not have consented to become the virgin mother of the Son of God, the Savior could not have been born and man's salvation would then have become impossible.

According to this peculiar idea, God's plan for the redemption of mankind hinged on Miriam's consent. As the spouse of the Holy Spirit, her place is above the human race and close to that of divinity. As a matter of fact, Miriam's place in Roman Catholic thought and devotion has gradually become transformed from a humble handmaid of God to that of a near deity, an idea which is pagan in origin and totally alien to Scripture and to the Spirit of God.

The question is, would God have entrusted Miriam with the high privilege of being the mother of the Messiah if she were minded to oppose His will? Would she have been worthy of God's favor? Miriam would have been altogether unworthy of God's high favor and He would have found a more worthy person to accomplish His purpose.

"Be it unto me according to thy word" was not an expression of consent on Miriam's part to the angel's annunciation, but rather an expression of humble submission to God's will.

"Be it unto me according to thy word" is what we would expect from a devout servant of God. There were many Jewish maidens who perhaps secretly cherished the dream of becoming the mother of the Messiah. But God in His sovereign wisdom bestowed this favor upon Miriam. The glory of Miriam rests not upon fatuous flights of fantasy or forced interpretations of Scripture, but solely upon the nobility of her faith and her glad submission to God's will. Such is the glory also of every true believer.

The Lukan narrative relating to the annunciation and to other incidents of the nativity breathes the spirit and atmosphere of the Old Testament. The setting of the events, the attitudes and reactions of the people involved in the drama of the incarnation, their mode of thinking, the very words they use are those which we might expect of Old Testament saints and heroes of the faith. Hannah, the mother of Samuel, would be a good example of this.

Miriam's reaction to the angelic annunciation, which is a challenge and a supreme test of her faith, is simple, noble, and worthy of a great daughter of Israel. In the galaxy of illustrious women of the Bible, Miriam's faith in God and her humility shine forth brightly as a star. To her the words of King Lemuel might be aptly applied: "Many daughters have done virtuously, but thou excellest them all" (Prov. 31:29).

CHAPTER SEVEN

Miriam and Elisabeth

And Mary arose in those days, and went into the hill country with haste, into a city of Judah; And entered into the house of Zacharias, and saluted Elisabeth.

And it came to pass, that, when Elisabeth heard the salutation of Mary, the babe leaped in her womb; and Elisabeth was filled with the Holy Ghost: And she spake out with a loud voice, and said, Blessed art thou among women, and blessed is the fruit of thy womb. And whence is this to me, that the mother of my Lord should come to me? For, lo, as soon as the voice of thy salutation sounded in mine ears, the babe leaped in my womb for joy. And blessed is she that believed: for there shall be a performance of those things which were told her from the Lord (Lk. 1:39–45)

W hen the angel Gabriel departed, it did not take Miriam very long to realize that God had already started to fulfill the message which the angel announced to her. Subtle, but very definite changes were beginning to take place in all her being. There was a quickening exultation within her which caused waves of joy and of somber reflection to reverberate within her soul. Was it possible that God would entrust so great a mystery, so high a privilege, and so ominous a responsibility to her, little Miriam, who not so long ago was only a *naarah*—a young girl?

She wanted to talk this over with someone dear who would understand and encourage her. But she hardly dared to do it. Her secret was too sacred, too precious to share with anyone. No, not even with her beloved Joseph. How could he believe her even if she did?

Miriam's situation as an expectant mother, though only betrothed to

Joseph, put her in a real predicament, if not in actual danger of being suspect of adultery, a crime punishable by stoning, according to the Law of Moses (Dt. 22:13–21). We must remember that Miriam was a daughter of a community whose sex standards were the highest among all the nations of the ancient world.

And then she remembered the angel's word about her kinswoman Elisabeth. Somehow in the providence of God, Elisabeth became inextricably involved in her own mystery. Only Elisabeth, herself the object of God's miraculous intervention, could possibly understand her. Only she could offer counsel and consolation in this awesome experience which had come into her young life.

And so Miriam hastened to visit Elisabeth.

Tradition has it that the home of Elisabeth and Zacharias, the parents of John the Baptist, was in Ain Kerem, a picturesque village in the hills of Judea, about five miles north of Jerusalem.

It was there that Miriam went to see her cousin Elisabeth. Encouraged by the angel's message, she decided to confide in Elisabeth, her kindred not only by family ties but also in spirit and in faith. Like Miriam, Elisabeth too belonged to that circle of devout Jewish women who were daily awaiting "the consolation of Israel." And so Miriam made her way a distance of some 80 miles from Nazareth to the vicinity of Jerusalem, a journey which proved to be a most rewarding and heartening experience for both women.

We can readily perceive with what eager animation and love the younger and older women greeted each other. Knowing something of the warm, outgoing nature of the children of Israel, we can readily reconstruct the meeting of the two kinswomen, brought even closer by the mystery of God's strange dealing with them.

We can visualize Miriam approaching her cousin first shyly, tears in her eyes and with outstretched arms. A pair of loving arms were only too ready to embrace her and to exchange the customary kiss of welcome and greeting *Shalom Alaich* (Peace be unto you). Both women reacted to each other from the depths of their overflowing hearts, so peculiarly tested by the mystery of divine condescension. Under the strain of profound emotion, Elisabeth felt her baby stir in her womb.

This is not the first time in biblical narrative that we are made aware of prenatal influences and the reactions on the part of yet unborn babes.

In Genesis 25:22–23, we read that the unborn twins of Rebekah, Esau and Jacob, clashed in her womb. "And the children struggled together within her; and she said, If it be so, why am I thus? And she went to enquire of the LORD. And the LORD said unto her, Two nations are in thy womb, and two manner of people shall be separated from thy bowels; and the one people shall be stronger than the other people; and the elder shall serve the younger."

It is interesting to read the comment on this passage by Rashi, one of the most famous Jewish biblical commentators of the 11th century: "The babes clashed. Esau wanted to come forth whenever she passed a temple of idols, whereas Jacob wanted to come forth whenever she passed a temple of God."[1]

The meaning of this quaint comment is that the nature and the destiny of man is already predetermined before his birth, even in the womb of his mother. The prophet Jeremiah expressed it this way: "Then the word of the LORD came unto me, saying, Before I formed thee in the belly I knew thee; and before thou camest forth out of the womb I sanctified thee, and I ordained thee a prophet unto the nations" (Jer. 1:4–5).

The child in Elisabeth's womb reacted in a similar manner, responding joyfully to the occasion.

> *And it came to pass, that, when Elisabeth heard the salutation of Mary, the babe leaped in her womb; and Elisabeth was filled with the Holy Ghost: And she spake out with a loud voice, and said, Blessed art thou among women, and blessed is the fruit of thy womb.*
>
> *And whence is this to me that the mother of my Lord should come to me? For, lo, as soon as the voice of thy salutation sounded in mine ears, the babe leaped in my womb for joy. And blessed is she that believed; for there shall be a performance of those things which were told her from the Lord* (Lk. 1:41–45).

Elisabeth's salutation to Miriam is filled with prophetic vision, joyful anticipation, and with the living messianic hope.

"BLESSED ART THOU AMONG WOMEN"

Such words were undoubtedly used upon momentous occasions as an expression of highest tribute. In a similar manner Ozias, king of Judah, greeted the legendary Judith, the heroic widow who, in order to rescue her nation, ventured her life and cut off the head of the Assyrian general, Holofernes:

> *Then said Ozias unto her, O daughter, blessed art thou of the most high God above all the women upon the earth; and blessed be the Lord God, which hath created the heavens and the earth, which hath directed thee to the cutting off of the head of the chief of our enemies.* [2]

Miriam was blessed among women because the fruit of her womb was blessed above all others.

It was a greeting of touching humility and joy, a recognition that Miriam's supreme merit was in the fact that she believed: "Blessed is she that believed." Miriam believed against everything that seemed rational, natural, or humanly possible.

The true greatness of Miriam was her faith in God's promise. Even as her illustrious ancestor Abraham believed "and it was accounted to him for righteousness," so did Miriam, thus proving that she too was a true and worthy daughter of her great forebear.

CHAPTER EIGHT

The Magnificat

*And Mary said, My soul doth magnify the Lord, and my spirit
hath rejoiced in God my Saviour, for he hath regarded the low
estate of his handmaiden: for, behold, from henceforth all generations shall call me blessed.*

*For he that is mighty hath done to me great things; and holy is his
name. And his mercy is on them that fear him from generation to
generation.He hath shewed strength with his arms; he hath scattered the proud in the imagination of their hearts.*

*He hath put down the mighty from their seats, and exalted them
of low degree. He hath filled the hungry with good things; and the
rich he hath sent empty away. He hath holpen his servant Israel, in
remembrance of his mercy; as he spake to our fathers, to Abraham,
and to his seed for ever* (Lk. 1:46-55)

It was the most natural thing for any daughter of Israel in the hour of
exultation and ecstasy to open her heart to God in a hymn of praise
couched in scriptural phraseology and imagery, and unconsciously
perhaps patterned after the psalms.

The characteristic form of Hebrew poetry, the parallelism, is evident
throughout the Magnificat. "My soul doth magnify the Lord, and my
spirit hath rejoiced in God my Saviour." Here we have even a triple
parallelism or correspondence of word and thought.

My soul—my spirit
doth magnify—hath rejoiced
doth magnify the Lord—hath rejoiced in God my Savior.

Miriam was reared in an atmosphere of piety which was steeped in biblical lore and in the messianic aspirations of those "who waited for the consolation of Israel." She could only express the deepest stirrings of her soul in terms familiar to her from close contacts with the Temple in Jerusalem, the synagogue in her native Nazareth, and her daily life among her countrymen.

Prayer and adoration were as natural to her as breathing and thinking. Ravaged by the oppression of the proud and mighty from within, and the scorn of the foreign rulers in the seat of the mighty from without, Galilean piety was warm and personal. It tended toward the practical and down-to-earth daily aspects of life rather than to the ritualistic and sacerdotal. Galilean religion was firmly rooted in the prophetic tradition. It was keenly sensitive to the wrongs endured by the common people.

It was not mere chance that Galilee had been, for many generations, the seedbed of revolts with strong patriotic, social, and messianic overtones. To these explosive Galileans, the messianic hope carried not only "end of time" expectations, but hopes for the immediate unseating of the mighty and proud, and for the lifting up from the dust of the poor and the humble.

The Magnificat, Miriam's hymn of praise, gives voice to all the ancient hopes and aspirations of her people.

There is a close resemblance in word and in theme between Miriam's song and the song of praise which 1,000 years before her, and under somewhat similar circumstances, another Jewish woman, Hannah, the mother of Samuel, sang:

> *My heart rejoiceth in the LORD, mine horn is exalted in the LORD: my mouth is enlarged over mine enemies; because I rejoice in thy salvation. There is none holy as the LORD: for there is none beside thee: neither is there any rock like our God. Talk no more so exceedingly proudly; let not arrogancy come out of your mouth: for the LORD is a God of knowledge, and by him actions are weighed.*

> *The bows of the mighty men are broken, and they that stumbled are girded with strength. They that were full have hired themselves for bread; and they that were hungry ceased: so that the barren hath born seven; and she that hath many children is waxed feeble* (1 Sam. 2:1–5).

No doubt Miriam would be familiar with Hannah's hymn of praise and, under similar circumstances, would give similar expression to that which stirred her own soul.

Miriam's hymn begins with an ascription of praise to God: "My soul doth magnify the Lord."

This reminds us of the *Kaddish*, the Mourner's Prayer, in the synagogue prayer book, which begins with the words: "May the name of the Lord be magnified and hallowed."

In a similar vein, the son of Miriam was to teach His disciples how to pray, "Our Father, which art in heaven, hallowed be thy name, thy kingdom come" (Mt. 6:9; Lk. 11:2).

"To magnify the Lord," to hallow His name is one of the most excellent forms of Hebrew prayer. It is praising God for what He is. This is pure adoration.

"And my spirit doth rejoice in God my Saviour."

Note the parallel: "*My* spirit doth rejoice in God *my* Saviour."

Hers was a most personal and intimate experience.

Protestant theologians make much of the phrase "God my Saviour" to prove that the mother of our Lord was a sinner and conscious of her need of a Savior. Undoubtedly Miriam, like every other human being, was a sinner. However, her words "God my Saviour" do not prove this. The psalmist's confession: "Behold I was shapen in iniquity, and in sin did my mother conceive me" (Ps. 51:5) applied to Miriam as to everyone born of a woman. The dogma of the Immaculate Conception is entirely alien to the teaching of the Scriptures.[1]

Catholic theologians, on the other hand, anxious to remove anything that might contradict their dogma of the Immaculate Conception and sinlessness of Mary, seek to explain away this same reference to "God my Saviour" as meaning that Mary rejoiced in God her Savior, that is Jesus, because being her Son, He belonged to her. She was therefore using the possessive "my." However, it seems to us that both interpretations, Catholic and Protestant, miss the true significance of this passage.

It must be remembered that the Magnificat is not a penitential psalm. Miriam does not set out to confess her sins either directly, or indirectly by implication. Her purpose is to magnify God, to extol His mighty deed, who has at last vindicated the hope of Israel, in bringing about the birth of the long-expected Messiah.

She extols and rejoices in God "her" Savior, not only as a daughter of Israel, but because "her" God has deigned to choose her, God's handmaiden, as a means to accomplish His holy purpose. There is a deep sense of gratitude to God for unmerited favor so richly bestowed upon her. "For he hath regarded the low estate of his handmaiden."

There is an awareness of the unsurpassed importance of the experience vouchsafed to her, "For, behold, from henceforth all generations shall call me blessed, for he that is mighty hath done to me great things."

Miriam lived in a world ruled by the mighty and contemptuous power of Rome, aided and abetted by the cruel house of Herod. To make the situation even more intolerable, Israel had to endure the burdens of its own self-seeking ecclesiastical hierarchy.[2] In addition, she was subject to the powerful, religious stranglehold of the Pharisees and the scribes ("who devour widows' houses and for a pretense make long prayer," Mt. 23:14). As a daughter of despised Galilee, she keenly anticipated that her supernatural child would bring about a total upheaval in the intolerable order of things.

"He has scattered the proud in the imagination of their hearts, he hath put down the mighty from their seats, and exalted them of low degree."

"The proud shall be humbled, and those of low degree shall be lifted up" is a part of the messianic vision which "the humble in Israel" have cherished from time immemorial. It finds an echo in Hannah's hymn of thanksgiving, and also in the words of the psalmist,

He raiseth up the poor out of the dust, and lifteth the needy out of the dunghill; that he may set him with princes, even with the princes of his people (Ps. 113:7–8).

Miriam's hymn especially articulates the longings of the despised and sorely tried people of Galilee and of all Israel: "He has filled the hungry with good things; and the rich he hath sent empty away."

Compassion for the poor, for the hungry, for the afflicted was very real in the home of Miriam and Joseph the carpenter. The atmosphere which prevailed in their godly home was steeped in biblical and prophetic lore. This was bound to have a profound effect on the spiritual and moral growth of the Child Jesus.

In the message of the Sermon on the Mount, later to be proclaimed by her divine son, we can hear distant echoes of His mother's hymn of praise:

Blessed are the poor in spirit: for theirs is the kingdom of heaven.
Blessed are they that mourn: for they shall be comforted.
Blessed are the meek: for they shall inherit the earth.
Blessed are they which do hunger and thirst after righteousness: for
they shall be filled.
Blessed are the merciful: for they shall obtain mercy.
Blessed are the pure in heart: for they shall see God (Mt. 5:3–8).

Miriam, at this moment of her inspired exaltation, was the personification of downtrodden, hungry, and thirsty Israel, ever waiting and hoping for "the consolation of Israel." The birth of her miracle child was about to initiate the fulfillment of all the hopes Israel had cherished since the days of Abraham and Jacob: "For thy salvation have I waited, O Lord" (Gen. 49:18). Now this hope was about to become flesh through this child which she, Miriam, blessed above all other women, carried in her womb.

"He hath holpen his servant Israel, in remembrance of his mercy; as he spake to our fathers, to Abraham, and to his seed for ever" (Lk. 1:54–55).

The Magnificat is in spirit, in sentiment, and in its expression, Old Testament prophecy, a link between ancient hope and the dawn of its fulfillment. It is the first Messianic hymn of the New Testament.

Miriam's hymn glorifies God for what He has already done and for what He is about to accomplish. Her glory is reflected in the glory of her son and of His Kingdom. She seeks nothing for herself but all for the glory of God.

Miriam was not only the chosen instrument of the incarnation, but the faithful witness and singer of the deliverance which God wrought through the fruit of her womb, Jesus.

CHAPTER NINE

The Birth of Jesus

And it came to pass in those days, that there went out a decree from Caesar Augustus, that all the world should be taxed. (And this taxing was first made when Cyrenius was governor of Syria.) And all went to be taxed, every one into his own city.

And Joseph also went up from Galilee, out of the city of Nazareth, into Judaea, unto the city of David, which is called Bethlehem; (because he was of the house and lineage of David), to be taxed with Mary his espoused wife, being great with child.

And so it was, that, while they were there, the days were accomplished that she should be delivered. And she brought forth her firstborn son, and wrapped him in swaddling clothes, and laid him in a manger; because there was no room for them in the inn (Lk. 2:1–7).

One of the most difficult problems relating to the birth of Jesus is to establish the exact date when this actually happened.

Although this problem does not concern us immediately, nevertheless, since the life of Jesus and of His mother were so intricately interrelated, we must of necessity give some attention to it.

Of one thing we can be reasonably sure: Christ was not born in the year AD 1. This date was simply a chronological mistake originated by a 6th-century monk, Dionysius Exiguus. It was he who selected the year of the incarnation as the turning point in history from which all events should be dated backward and forward. Exiguus assumed the birth of our Lord to be December 25, probably relying on a contemporary tradition among Christians.

Although the exact date of the birth of Jesus cannot be established with complete accuracy, yet within narrow limits there is general agreement among biblical historians that it occurred approximately toward the end of the year 5 BC. Some date it a year or more earlier.

The evidences concerning this matter are of an internal or external nature.

The internal evidences are references to the birth of Christ in the New Testament.

The external evidences are statements relating to Christ made by secular historians of the first century such as Josephus, Tacitus, Seutonius, and Pliny the Younger. These references appear in most of the standard works dealing with the life of Christ.

In the Gospel of Luke we find more historical details and data concerning Miriam and Jesus than in any other Gospel. Luke the evangelist is obviously at pains to relate his data and to coordinate them with important events in contemporary history.

The question is, how reliable a historian was the evangelist Luke? He himself assures us that his material came to him from the accounts of eyewitnesses, and that he has set forth their accounts methodically and with great care [akriboos] (1:1–4).

Until fairly recently, it was fashionable to treat lightly Luke's accuracy as a historian. However, archaeological discoveries of recent times have amazingly enhanced and confirmed his reliability.

The noted scholar, Sir William Ramsay, stated: "Luke is a historian of first rank. Not merely are his statements of fact trustworthy, he is possessed of the true historic sense....In short, the author should be placed along with the very greatest of historians."[1]

According to Luke, the birth of Jesus took place at the time when Caesar Augustus (30 BC-AD 14) decreed "that all the world should be taxed." The term for *world* used by Luke, *oikoumene*, means the inhabited Roman world (2:1).

From the papyri documents discovered in Egypt in recent years it has been established that every 14 years the Roman government conducted a general count of its population for purposes of taxation. To avoid confusion and duplications, every person was obliged to register in his native town. The first such count took place when Cyrenius (Quirinius) was governor of Syria (v. 2).

It has been further established on the basis of ancient documents that this first poll ordered by Caesar Augustus took place in the year 8 BC. Due to political difficulties in Palestine it is likely that the census was delayed for perhaps as long as one to three years. This time would coincide with the time of the birth of our Lord.

From a reference by Josephus[2] we learn that, shortly before his death, Herod the Great executed several prominent leaders and that, on that same night, an eclipse of the moon occurred. Astronomical calculations have indicated that on the night of March 12 or 13, 4 BC, a partial eclipse of the moon actually did take place. Herod died before the Passover of 4 BC, which in that year happened to be April 12. The events described in the Gospels of Matthew and Luke must at least have taken about two to three months and perhaps considerably longer, if allowance is made for the flight of the holy family to Egypt. This would set the date of the birth of Christ at least toward the end of 5 BC, at the earliest. The traditional date of the nativity, December 25, cannot be proved or disproved. It may however rest on some ancient tradition handed down from generation to generation. The festive celebration of the Saturnalia, observed by Romans on December 25, may or may not have a bearing on the traditional date of Christmas.

The oft-repeated argument advanced against December 25 as the date of the nativity, that shepherds would not keep their sheep out in the fields during the winter is, in our opinion, not tenable. In the vicinity of Bethlehem the winters are usually quite mild. From this writer's own experience in Northeastern Europe, where winters are much colder, it is certain that sheep are permitted to graze in the fields even during a frost, let alone during a mild winter. In the night the sheep may have been sheltered in the natural caves outside Bethlehem, while the shepherds kept watch over them.

Of some further interest regarding the fixing of the nativity date is the reference by Tacitus, the Roman historian of the first century, who when describing the burning of Rome in the year 64 AD, mentions the Christians as being suspected of starting the fire. In this connection he explains the origin of the name "Christian" by saying, "They received their name from Christ who was executed by the procurator Pontius Pilate when Tiberius was emperor."[3] Pontius Pilate was procurater of

Palestine during AD 26-36.[4] It was during his term of office that Jesus
was condemned to die on the cross, at the age of about 33 years.

WHERE WAS JESUS BORN?

On this point the New Testament is clear and definite: Jesus was born
in Bethlehem (Mt. 2:1, 6, 8; Lk. 2:4). From time to time there have
been those who sought to impugn the reliability of the New Testament account and suggested that Jesus was born, not in Bethlehem,
but in Nazareth. The fact that Jesus was referred to as the Nazarene
and His followers were called Nazarenes has been cited in support of
this theory.[5] However, the fact that Nazareth was the home of Jesus,
where He spent the first 30 years of His life before entering upon His
ministry, is sufficient to account for this.

Luke's description of the nativity suggests that when God's appointed
hour had struck, the seemingly inauspicious birth of an unknown, yet
long-predicted child of a despised race in little Bethlehem and the decree
of a mighty ruler of Rome converged to accomplish the divine purpose.

"In the fullness of time," the governor of Syria decreed a census in
his province and Joseph and Miriam had to undertake the arduous
journey to their ancestral home, at the very time when Miriam's "days
were accomplished" in order that Jesus might be born in Bethlehem,
so that the ancient prophecy of Micah might be fulfilled:

> But thou, Bethlehem Ephrathah, though thou be little among the
> thousands of Judah, yet out of thee shall he come forth unto me that
> is to be the ruler in Israel; whose goings forth have been from of old,
> from everlasting (Mic. 5:2).

SHEPHERDS OF BETHLEHEM

Bethelehem was, in the days of Miriam, the generally accepted birthplace
of the Messiah in accordance with Micah's prophecy.

In the Pseudo-Jonathan Targum (an Aramaic paraphrase of the
Pentateuch), on Genesis 35:21, we read: "'And Israel journeyed, and
spread his tent beyond the tower of Edar.' This refers to the Messiah,
that He was to be born in Bethlehem and to be revealed from Migdal
Edar, which means the tower of the flock."

This brings to memory the story of the shepherds, who were watching their flocks on the hills of Judea. Edersheim suggests that these shepherds were not ordinary shepherds but special watchmen appointed by the Temple authorities to watch over the flocks of sheep that were destined for sacrifice in the Temple. These flocks lay out on the hills all year round, even in the winter.

It is interesting to note that December 25 (the 9th of Tebeth) is considered by pious Jews a fast day. The reason for this fast is not clear. It is probable that this is some cryptic allusion to the birth of Jesus on December 25.[6] That the Jews should consider the birthday of Jesus an occasion for fasting, is not so much a reflection of their hostility to Him, but rather an expression of their experiences with medieval Christianity.

THE INN OF BETHLEHEM

The inn referred to in the Gospel narrative was probably like some of the still-extant inns in Bible lands, a square enclosure open to the sky, surrounded by a wooden porch and a few rooms, available for rental to travelers. Even today one can see such an inn in Nazareth. An ancient tradition maintains that the animal shelter was located in a cave in which the hills near Bethlehem abound. The Church of the Nativity in Bethlehem is believed to have been built over the cave where Miriam brought forth her firstborn.

In the Lukan account of the nativity we see the hand of God at work imperceptibly, intricately weaving together the strands of human events into the grand design of His eternal purpose, which is the redemption of man. How subtly and masterfully this point is suggested by the evangelist.

The throne of Caesar Augustus and the manger in Bethlehem stand in stark contrast to each other: The poor, the despised, and the foolish things of God are used to confound and to put to naught that which is rich, powerful, and wise in the eyes of the world.

"In the fullness of time" the dried up and almost forgotten branch of the house of David in the person of the little child returns to its ancestral home in Bethlehem to initiate the Kingdom of God in the hearts of men, and eventually to break in pieces the kingdoms of this world (Ps. 2:4–7).

There is also a hint of subtle irony in the nativity story: Miriam, "great with child," and her weary, anxious husband Joseph could find no room in the inn of Bethlehem.

There was no place of shelter for the Savior of Israel in any human habitation, only a cave for cattle and a rude manger. When Miriam's hour came, there were no comforting, gentle, womanly hands to ease her birthpangs. Such was the birth of Him who was to become the "despised and rejected" Savior of men.

THE PIERCING SWORD

What were the thoughts which crossed the mind of Miriam as she labored in pain to deliver her firstborn, we shall never know. Miriam was a woman given to pondering and contemplation.

A corner of the veil of mystery had been lifted for her by the angel. Yet much about this baby which she had "wrapped in swaddling clothes and laid in the manger" was still mysterious and inscrutable. There were many hard lessons laid up in store for Miriam which would pierce her soul, and deeply wound her maternal instincts and love for this miraculous child of hers.

Beside the disbelief and suspicion on the part of the community of which she was a part, there would also be a ceaseless conflict within her own soul. For Miriam was no plaster saint, nor a painted, frozen image upon a stained glass window in a dim Gothic church, but a warm, vibrant, sensitive human being of flesh and blood, with many disturbing thoughts on her mind, pressing for an answer.

That which happened was too overwhelming for her, or for any human being to comprehend fully. In spite of the angel's annunciation and Elisabeth's homage to her yet unborn child, in some ways it must have been more difficult for Miriam than for almost anybody else to grasp the magnitude of the mystery of the incarnation and its transcendent significance.

How could she, Miriam, almost a child herself, comprehend that this helpless little baby nestling in her arms, which she nourished with her breast and for whose every physical need she had to care like any other mother, would one day be the glorious Messiah, the focus of all the fervent hopes of Israel and the yearnings of humanity?

"How shall this be?" was a question she had asked the angel at the annunciation but which she would ask herself repeatedly in the

THE BIRTH OF JESUS

intimacy of her soul.

Miriam, the tender flower of Jewish womanhood, would always be subject to that constant tension between her abiding faith in God and her inquiring mind which demanded an answer to the question "How shall this be?"

Within her sensitive and loving heart there must have been the strange and foreboding premonition that her beloved child, destined by the decree of heaven for greatness, would also have to endure great suffering and agony of soul. That His path would one day lead to Calvary and a cross could hardly have been within sight of her immediate horizon. True, there were familiar Scriptures like Isaiah 53 and Psalm 22 and old traditions which spoke of a suffering deliverer, but she could as yet hardly have discerned what bearing all this would have upon this precious bundle of life within her arms.

However, the amazing events which preceded and followed the birth of her wondrous child stirred up hopes and fears, thrilling anticipations and numbing fears within her whole being. For Miriam was the kind of woman who "kept all these things, and pondered them in her heart" (Lk. 2:19).

Now and again we shall see a hint of this inner conflict in the Gospels, a conflict which was never quite resolved during the earthly pilgrimage of her beloved son. Only after His resurrection, when she found herself, together with His brothers, in the company of the apostles and the first believers in the upper room in Jerusalem, came the final answer and the complete victory of faith.

Throughout the ensuing centuries a legion of artists have made the mother of Jesus the subject of their art, giving expression in numerous forms to their vision of her. Most artists have presented to the world a stereotoyped, stylized, and lifeless image of the virgin mother. There is, however, one painting which I remember from my youth.

In this picture, the child Jesus is bedded down on a carpenter's workbench, serene and happy. His youthful mother, in a loving gesture, holds the baby's right hand up to her lips. Her brooding eyes, looking into the distance, are brimming over with tears and nameless forebodings, as if sensing the thorny road of her beloved child, the road which will eventually lead to Calvary.

That artist knew something of Miriam's love, her sorrow, and her fears.

Between the crib and the cross, the sword often pierced her soul, even as the angel of God foretold. At such times Miriam's only shield was the shield of every believing heart—her faith in God and His promises.

CHAPTER TEN

The Ancestry of Miriam and Joseph

THE IMPORTANCE OF GENEALOGICAL RECORDS

Genealogy, or the tracing of the ancestry of a person or a family, held a vital place in the life of ancient Israel. On the correct genealogy depended the succession to the royal throne, to the priesthood, and Levitical order with all its responsibilities and dignity, or to the headship of a family and the right of inheritance. Even more than wealth, the splendor or obscurity of one's family tree played a role in marriage.

Genealogical records were kept among the Jews since olden times (Num. 1:2, 18 and 1 Chr. 5:7, 17). The Talmud asserts that Ezra the Scribe would not leave Babylon until he had succeeded in sifting the genealogical records of Israel to a degree resembling that of the finest flour.[1]

When, in the days of Ezra, certain priests were unable to prove their unimpaired priestly descent by producing proper genealogies, they were considered polluted and were removed from the priesthood (Ezra 2:61–63). In Ezra 2—5 and Nehemiah 7—10, the heads of the families of those who returned under Zerubbabel from Babylon to Judah and Jerusalem are enumerated. These lists must have been based on genealogical records which were already in existence at that time and jealously guarded in later generations.

Official records and genealogies were undoubtedly kept in the archives of the Temple in Jerusalem, and also by the royal court. Individual families, especially those who made claim to some notable persons among their ancestry, jealously guarded family records like a priceless jewel.

Family pride was often deeply involved in the preservation and the searching of such records. (It also often led to genealogical misrepresentations.) It has been stated that 900 camel loads of commentaries

existed just on the genealogies in 1 Chronicles.[2] Pride of descent—
yihus—was so highly regarded that a marriage could be annulled if
proven *yihus*—descent register—had been manipulated.

(Even today such genealogies, often purporting to go back to ancient
days, are occasionally preserved among prominent Jewish families. For
religious purposes the Jews still divide their people in three groups, the
priests, the Levites, and common Israelites.)

The Herods, who had a morbid suspicion of anyone who might lay
claim to the throne of David, not only did away, whenever possible,
with physical descendants of the royal family, but sought to obliterate
their genealogical records. Nevertheless, family genealogies were still
too fresh in the minds of the people and too well preserved in public
and private documents for these to be altogether destroyed.

In the case of Jesus, the Davidic descent of one or both of His
presumed parents was undoubtedly a well-established fact, based on
existing documents and tradition jealously guarded and handed down
from generation to generation. It is interesting to note that His Davidic
descent was never questioned by His contemporaries, but was generally
taken for granted and acclaimed (Mt. 21:9,15; Mk. 11:9,10; Jn. 12:13).

THE GENEALOGY OF JESUS

In the New Testament we have two genealogies of Christ, in Matthew
and in Luke. Matthew 1:1–16 gives the order of descendants from
Abraham to David, then from David to the Babylonian captivity, and
from the Babylonian captivity to Christ. For the purpose of symmetry
and easy remembrance, each period is divided into 14 generations.

Apparently, Matthew's primary purpose was to present Jesus both
as the lawful descendant to the throne of David, and the fulfiller of the
divine promise to Abraham that "in thee shall all families of the earth
be blessed" (Gen. 12:3). Luke 3:23–38 gives us the genealogy of Christ
in reverse. He begins with Jesus, the Son of God begotten of the Holy
Spirit, the second Adam, as distinguished from the first Adam, who was
the son of God by creation. The two genealogies differ in a number of
details. These differences have challenged Christian writers throughout
the centuries. The most important difference is that in Matthew, Joseph
appears to be "the son of Jacob," whereas in Luke, Joseph is designated
as "the son of Heli."

Admittedly this is a serious difficulty, which cannot be easily dissolved after a period of nearly 20 centuries.

There are several schools of thought concerning these genealogical differences: One, which goes back to the third century, maintains that both tables are the genealogy of Joseph, and that Heli and Jacob were half-brothers, having the same father, called by Matthew "Matthan" and by Luke "Matthat," but born of different mothers.

When Heli died childless, Jacob, in accordance with the law of levirate marriage (Dt. 25:5), took his widow to wife and "raised up seed" to his brother Heli by begetting a son, Joseph. In this way Matthew could say, "Matthan begat Jacob, and Jacob begat Joseph." And Luke could write, "Joseph, which was the son of Heli, which was the son of Matthat." Both records were therefore equally true, although on the surface they seem to differ.

Another solution is suggested by the assumption that Matthew gives the legal successors to the throne of David while Luke gives the paternal ancestors of Joseph. The line of Solomon became extinct in Jechoniah, also known as Jehoiachin. From that time on, the succession passed over to the collateral line through Nathan, the son of David.

For a brief space the royal line and the natural lineage of Joseph were identical. But after the days of Zerubbabel the two lines separated. The family of the elder son, in whom the title to the throne was vested, became extinct. After that, the descendants of the younger son succeeded to the title, and Matthat or Matthan became heir apparent.

According to this line of thought it is assumed that Matthat or Matthan had two sons, Jacob and Heli. Jacob had no son but a daughter, the virgin Miriam. The younger brother Heli had a son Joseph. As his uncle Jacob had no male descendant, Joseph became the legitimate heir to the throne of David.

Generally, since the times of the Reformation, the preponderance of opinion has been among Bible scholars that Matthew gives the genealogy of Joseph and proves him to be the heir to the throne of David; whereas Luke gives the genealogy of Miriam and shows Jesus to be an actual descendant of David.

Thus, the Davidic descent of Jesus is established legally through Matthew and physically through Miriam, a lineal descendant of David.[3]

An interesting sidelight is afforded to us in Numbers 36:6–10. There the Lord commanded that, in the absence of male heirs, heiresses should marry "only to the family of their tribe of their father" in order that "the inheritance shall not be removed from tribe to tribe."

While this law applies only to heiresses, yet it is reasonable to assume that such a law would tend to establish a strong tradition of marrying within the ranks of the same tribe. In fact, we know from the Talmud that there was a definite trend among Jews to marry within the tribe and within the social sphere of the prospective spouse.

In this way it may be reasonably assumed that Miriam was a descendant of the house of David, in accordance with the oldest Christian tradition.

Very clearly the New Testament writers uniformly present Jesus as a physical descendant of David and heir to his throne. All things considered, there can be no valid reason to impugn their statements (Mt. 22:41–42; Lk. 1:32; Acts 2:25–36; 13:22–23; Rom. 1:3; 2 Tim. 2:8; Rev. 5:5; 22:16).

MIRIAM IN THE APOCRYPHAL "NEW TESTAMENT "

The apocryphal "New Testament" writings add nothing to our sure knowledge of the background of Miriam. The so-called Infancy Gospels, as usual, provide us with a mass of legendary stories and fables about Miriam and Joseph and the childhood of Jesus and His home life.

In the apocryphal Book of James, also known as the Protevangelium, Miriam's parents are called Ioachim and Anna. We are told that Anna was barren and bewailed her childlessness. She prayed to God in these words: "O God of our Fathers, bless me and hearken unto my prayer, as Thou didst bless the womb of Sara and gavest her a son, even Isaac."

In answer to this prayer an angel of the Lord appeared to her and said, "Anna, Anna, the Lord has hearkened unto thy prayer, and thou shalt conceive and bear, and thy seed shall be spoken of in the whole world."

In due course Anna gave birth to a baby girl and called her name Mary. She dedicated her child to the Lord and, when it was two years old, it was brought to the Temple and nurtured by an angel.

When Miriam was 12 years old, the priests held a council saying, "Behold Mary is become twelve years old in the Temple of the Lord. What then shall we do with her lest she pollute the sanctuary of the Lord?"

The high priest Zacharias entered the Holy of Holies and prayed for guidance. In answer, the Lord sent an angel who commanded Zacharias to assemble all the widowers of Judea, every one to bring a rod, and to whomsoever the rod should show a sign his wife should she be. The sign was given to Joseph: A dove came and sat on his rod. Reluctantly, Joseph, who was already advanced in age, was persuaded by the high priest to take Mary as his wife, but he did not live with her as husband and wife. A little later, Mary was selected from among seven virgins of the house of David to weave a veil for the Temple of the Lord. At the time of the annunciation Mary was 16 years old.[4]

Such are some of the legendary stories which have come down to us in the so-called apocryphal Gospels such as the Gospel of Pseudo-Matthew, the Gospel of the Birth of Mary, the Gospel of Thomas, and in a great many others. These so-called Gospels were the principal source of inspiration for the artists and poets of the Middle Ages. From these sources medieval Christendom drew nurture for its insatiable curiosity concerning the intimate details connected with the life of Miriam, Joseph, and Jesus.

These apocryphal stories served as a foundation for the many nativity and passion plays so popular in the Middle Ages. However, the apocryphal writings, so rich in fables, folklore, and fantasy, were rightly rejected by the Christian church as unreliable records, often entirely unworthy of the message and person of Christ.

The oldest of these apocryphal Gospels, which is probably the Book of James, goes back to the early part of the second century. The apocryphal Gospels, acts, epistles and revelations, usually fashioned after the authentic New Testament writings, became more and more fanciful the farther they became removed from the scene of the events which they purported to describe, and from the times when these events were supposed to have taken place. Where knowledge failed, human imagination and ingenuity took over.

"HER FIRSTBORN SON"

Since it will be necessary for us later to consider the question whether Miriam had other children besides Jesus, we must analyze the term *firstborn* as used in Luke 2:7, "And she brought forth her firstborn son."

The Greek word is *prototokos,* which means literally "the firstborn," and is obviously a translation of the Hebrew word *b'chor*. This word signifies a firstborn male offspring, but not necessarily an only one. This distinction will become significant when we discuss later whether Miriam had only one child, or whether she was the mother of other children beside Jesus. Here it is sufficient to record that neither the Greek nor the Hebrew term for firstborn precludes other children.

It is interesting to note that, in the story of the binding of Isaac in Genesis 22, God addresses Himself to Abraham with the words "Take now thy son, thine only son Isaac, whom thou lovest" (v. 2). The Hebrew term for "only son" is *ben yachid*.

The Greek word for an "only one" is *monos,* and is so used in the Septuagint. The term *only begotten* used in John 3:16, "For God so loved the world that he gave his only begotten son," is in the Greek *monogenes*. This indicates supernatural origin and should not be confused with the word *firstborn*, as used in our text.

MIRIAM AND JOSEPH AS HUSBAND AND WIFE

The details of the relationship between Miriam and Joseph are, in the providence of God, veiled in the mantle of mystery. Their place in the Gospel narrative is subordinated to the central position of Miriam's supernatural son, Jesus. First Joseph, and later Miriam fade out of our view. Jesus alone remains to hold our attention. This was apparently the intention of the inspired writers of the New Testament records.

In Matthew 1:20–25 we read that the angel (most likely the angel of the annunciation, Gabriel) had to reassure Joseph not to fear to take Miriam to wife despite her condition, because she had conceived of the Holy Spirit and would bear a child whose name was to be Jesus, "for he shall save his people from their sins."[5]

Matthew 1:24 ("and took unto him his wife; and knew her not till she had brought forth her firstborn son") is one of the key passages in the Gospel. On its right interpretation depends our thinking concerning Miriam and her position in Christian thought and worship.

In general, the Protestant school of thought adheres to the literal interpretation of Matthew 1:24, that Joseph "knew her not till she brought forth her firstborn son." The obvious implication is that he "knew" Miriam as his wife after she gave birth to Jesus. In other words, that they lived normally as husband and wife.

The other view is the one vigorously defended by many that Joseph never "knew" Miriam as his wife. That is, that they never lived as husband and wife, and consequently they had no other children than Jesus.

Let us admit that the text as it stands, in itself, permits both interpretations. Nevertheless the New Testament record strongly favors the literal interpretation of Matthew 1:24, for the following reasons:

If Joseph never was the husband of Miriam in the common sense of the word, Scripture would not have failed to be explicit. This is too important a point to be left to the vagaries of human interpretations or misinterpretation.

In the absence of clear and compelling reasons, it is always a sound rule of scriptural exegesis to consider the common sense to be the true sense.

In view of the numerous references in the Gospels and also in the Acts of the Apostles to "the brothers and sisters" of Jesus, without any qualifying explanations, there is a strong presupposition that Joseph and Miriam were, after the birth of Jesus, in actual fact husband and wife, and that they had both sons and daughters, as mentioned in the Gospels (Mt. 13:55–56; Mk. 6:3).

There is also this additional consideration that Jewish piety and religious thought looked upon normal marital relations, for the purpose of raising children, as a praiseworthy obedience to God's commandment given to the first parents of the human race, "Be ye fruitful and multiply" (Gen. 9:1).

Celibacy has never been a Jewish ideal; in fact, it runs contrary to the whole spirit of the Old Testament.

The Jewish ideal is a family blessed with many children.

Lo, children are an heritage of the LORD: and the fruit of the womb is his reward. As arrows are in the hand of a mighty man; so are children of the youth. Happy is the man that hath his quiver full of them: they shall not be ashamed, but they shall speak with the enemies in the gate (Ps. 127:3–5).

Motherhood is considered a mark of divine favor: "He maketh the barren woman to keep house, and to be a joyful mother of children. Praise ye the LORD" (Ps. 113:9).

We know what agony of spirit many of the Hebrew women experienced when the Lord denied them the privilege of motherhood. Sarah, Rachel, Hannah, in the Old Testament, and Elisabeth in the New are examples of this.

After Jesus was born of the Holy Spirit, there was no reason whatsoever why Miriam and Joseph should not live as husband and wife. On the contrary, everything in the New Testament record points to the fact that they did.

CHAPTER ELEVEN

The Purification and Presentation

Miriam and Joseph acted in complete accordance with the Law of Moses (Lev. 12:1–8). The Child Jesus was duly circumcised the eighth day, and 33 days after that Miriam duly presented herself at the door of the Temple in Jerusalem, where the priest was to make an atoning sacrifice for the young mother, as a sign that her time of purification was completed and that she was now permitted to resume her lawful place in the community of Israel. During the time of her uncleanness she was not allowed to touch anything sacred nor to appear in the sanctuary.

The sacrifice ordinarily consisted of a lamb, but in the case of the poor, two turtle doves or pigeons.

> *And if she be not able to bring a lamb, then she shall bring two turtles, or two young pigeons; the one for the burnt-offering, and the other for a sin-offering: and the priest shall make an atonement for her, and she shall be clean* (Lev. 12:8).

One pigeon was a thanksgiving offering; the other an atoning sacrifice.

Rabbinical regulations allowed the mother to bring a monetary equivalent of the price of the pigeons. A large stock of these pigeons was kept in the Temple for just such occasions. The incident in the Temple, when Jesus "cast out all of them that sold and bought in the temple," and turned over "the seats of them that sold doves" is undoubtedly connected with this ritual (Mt. 21:12).

There are two things that we can assume from the story of Miriam's purification:

1. She considered herself just like any other Jewish mother, a sinner who needed an atoning sacrifice. Any thought to the contrary, such as the dogma of her Immaculate Conception, would have been to her utterly abhorrent.

2. The fact that she brought a pair of turtle doves or pigeons indicates that the family was in reduced material circumstances and could not afford a lamb which, in any case, did not cost very much.

THE PRESENTATION OF THE CHILD

Connected with the purification of the mother was the ceremony of the presentation of the child Jesus in the Temple. This too was in accordance with the Law of Moses (Ex. 13:1–2). Every firstborn in Israel, man and beast, belonged to the Lord. This commemorated the fact that all the firstborn, man and beast, were slain when God's wrath was poured out on Pharaoh and his people.

The ceremony of presentation of the child before God is preserved even to the present day among the Jews, although, due to the changed circumstances, in a residual form. Nowadays, it is called *pidion ha-ben*— the redemption of the son.

Usually 18 silver dollars, or whatever coin of the realm is used in the country, are presented as "ransom" to a *cohen*, a priest of the tribe of Levi. This ransom money of 18 silver coins is an old tradition because 18 is the Hebrew numerical equivalent of the word *chai*, which means "to live." (The author recently learned an amusing incident where a Jewish man, who happened to be a *cohen*, received the ransom money of 18 silver dollars, only to have them claimed back by the family when they realized that he was a Hebrew Christian.)

The story of the presentation of the child Jesus and Simeon's reception of the baby Jesus in the Temple is one of the most beautiful and touching narratives in the New Testament. The scene has been the subject of numerous paintings by the great artists of the past.

SIMEON

In the person of Simeon we have a representative of the priestly office at its spiritual best. Too often, the priestly clan had become rather inured to the deeper realities of their calling. Many of them had degenerated to the level of routine functionaries of a cult. Vested interest and pride of place had exerted its pernicious influence, even as it has done to the high practitioners of other religious cults. Since the times of the Maccabees, the high priesthood has been an object of barter and unseemly rivalry, not dissimilar to certain events in the later history of the church. The majority of the priests were Sadducees, but some were Pharisees.

Yet, even in the darkest hours, there was always a saving remnant in their midst who never lost the sense of their high calling, as mediators between God and His people. Such a Spirit-filled man was Simeon. He was able to discern these things which were hidden to those whose religion was primarily a matter of outward observances or of rites. Simeon belonged to the small group of those who fervently waited for the "consolation of Israel."

And, behold, there was a man in Jerusalem, whose name was Simeon; and the same man was just and devout, waiting for the consolation of Israel: and the Holy Ghost was upon him. And it was revealed unto him by the Holy Ghost, that he should not see death, before he had seen the Lord's Christ.

And he came by the Spirit into the temple: and when the parents brought in the child Jesus, to do for him after the custom of the law, then took he him up in his arms, and blessed God, and said, Lord, now lettest thou thy servant depart in peace, according to thy word: For mine eyes have seen thy salvation, which thou hast prepared before the face of all people; a light to lighten the Gentiles, and the glory of thy people Israel (Lk. 2:25–32).

Joseph and Miriam listened while the raptured priest blessed the child. The words of Simeon concerning this child surpassed in grandeur and majesty anything that was ever said about any child which was born of a woman.

We can imagine the aged Simeon waiting anxiously for the birth of the Messiah. Every time a child was brought to him to be blessed and "redeemed" his heart must have beaten expectantly: "Is this perhaps the child?" he would ask the Lord. "No, not yet, Simeon. Wait."

When the parents of Jesus brought the child "to do for him after the custom of the law" (Lk. 2:27), Simeon knew beyond any doubt that this was the long-expected child which the prophet foretold:

> *For unto us a child is born, unto us a son is given: and the gov-*
> *ernment shall be upon his shoulder: and his name shall be called*
> *Wonderful, Counselor, The Mighty God, The Everlasting Father,*
> *The Prince of Peace* (Isa. 9:6).

Something inexpressible but very real about Joseph and Miriam
and the child Himself confirmed to him that which the Holy Spirit of
God had revealed to him, that this was *the* child.

When Simeon, in the solemnity of the Temple, whispered to the
parents, as he must have done before, on numerous other occasions:
"What is the name of the child?" and when the whispered answer came
back: "Yeshua" (which means salvation), the heart of the priest was filled
with unspeakable joy and he exclaimed: "Now lettest thou thy servant
depart in peace, according to thy word: for mine eyes have seen thy
Salvation—thy Yeshuah—thy Jesus—a light to lighten the Gentiles,
and the glory of thy people Israel."

Such was the destiny of this divine child, and the ages yet unrealized
were to confirm its truth. Countless generations yet unborn would
confirm in their lives this awe-inspiring prophecy. Nothing that ever
happened to Israel in its remarkable career across the millennia ever
surpassed this claim to glory, that Jesus was born of a Jewish mother,
Miriam.

Of course Joseph and Miriam marveled at those things. Only
gradually could they get used to the thought that this baby was to be
more wonderful and excel in glory and cosmic significance than any
other baby which was ever born. They hardly dared hope that all these
marvelous things which they heard from angelic and human messengers
of God would really come to pass; that all this should happen to them,
the plain carpenter of Nazareth and his young wife, Miriam.

Their understanding of their child, Jesus, was, of necessity, a gradual
process. The immensity of the trust committed to them was too great
for their immediate comprehension. Miriam and Joseph were learning
about Jesus only step by step. They continued their education for the
rest of their lives as they went along with Him. Every day and every
experience brought home to them a new lesson, revealing to them, and

especially to Miriam, the immensity of the stature of this child which God had seen fit to entrust to them.

Simeon blessed Miriam and her husband Joseph, and said to the mother of Jesus:

Behold, this child is set for the fall and rising again of many in Israel; and for a sign which shall be spoken against; (Yea, a sword shall pierce through thy own soul also), that the thoughts of many hearts may be revealed (Lk. 2:34–35).

This prophecy of Simeon has come to pass in every generation and in every century. Jesus was indeed "set for the fall and rising again of many in Israel." Indeed many in Israel stumbled and fell because of Him. No other one has lifted up so many and made them children of God, as has this child of Miriam. No other person has ever provoked as much controversy, bitterness, and outright hatred as did Jesus. No one ever evoked more love, devotion, and blessedness beyond comprehension than did Jesus.

SWORD THRUSTS

The sword which pierced Miriam was a sword of suffering and travail which is not easy to understand except by careful and empathetic understanding of this vulnerable young virgin mother. Many were the thrusts which pierced her heart. The whispering and the taunts of neighbors and relatives and of so-called friends. Even her own Joseph, just man that he was, stumbled at her condition. At one time he even thought of putting her away privately. Divine intervention was necessary to change his plan.

The mystery of the incarnation, defying all nature and human experience, to which in the providence of God Miriam was made privy, was too staggering to be accepted by the people. Only a few choice souls could believe her amazing experience. The multitudes would scorn her and make her the laughingstock of their ribald jokes, or nudge one another knowingly, as she passed them by.

Then there was the overwhelming sense of the responsibility to which God had called her. To her was entrusted the mothering and the rearing of this divine child, a terrifying responsibility for one so humble. How was she to reveal to Him concerning His supernatural origin? How much could she reveal of her secret to her nearest kin or to strangers? How could they understand? These are only a few of the sword thrusts that pierced her faithful, loving heart.

As the years went by and her gradual understanding of the divine stature of her son grew, her perplexity and anxiety must have grown apace. The proximity of that which is divine and that which is human must, of necessity, create tensions almost beyond endurance. The most grievous and climactic sword thrust which went straight to her bleeding and broken heart was inflicted upon her when she stood helpless beneath the criminal's gibbet on which her innocent but crucified son was dying.

THE CONSOLATION OF ISRAEL

"And, behold, there was a man in Jerusalem, whose name was Simeon; and the same man was just and devout, waiting for the consolation of Israel: and the Holy Ghost was upon him" (v. 25).

The word *consolation* (in Hebrew, *nechamah*) has a peculiar eschatological and Messianic significance. It is a companion word to "salvation" or "redemption" and has a similar connotation.

The relationship between the idea of "salvation" (in Hebrew, *Yeshuah*) and "consolation" is like that between cause and effect. God causes salvation. Its effect is consolation for God's people. Consolation is the hope of Israel which has become a reality.

In Isaiah 49:13 we read, "For the LORD hath comforted his people and will have mercy upon his afflicted." In paraphrasing this passage, the Aramaic Targum says: "In the future, that is, in Messiah's time, Jehovah will comfort his people."

The term *consolation of Israel* became one of those meaningful phrases laden with the whole weight of Messianic expectation.

In the Apocalypse of Baruch 44:7 we read, "If you patiently continue in his worship and do not forget his law then will your times turn into salvation and you will see the consolation of Zion." In the Jerusalem Talmud, Bereshith Rabbah, on Genesis 1:21, there is this comment: "Jehovah created the great sea monsters, the Leviathan, and his mate for 'the day of consolation' (that is, for the feast of the righteous in the days of the Messiah)."[1]

The expression *consolation of Israel* was used among the Jews as a solemn oath, to confirm the veracity of one's words. It was just as if one would swear by God or by heaven. The consolation of Israel is the highest form of earthly bliss which the Jewish people hoped and prayed for through the centuries. Its realization was to take place when Messiah would come.

MESSIAH THE COMFORTER

It is significant that one of the names of the Messiah, according to the rabbis, is *Menachem,* which means the "consoler" or "comforter." In the light of this, it is interesting to read the words of our Lord in John 16:7, "Nevertheless I tell you the truth; it is expedient for you that I go away: for if I go not away, the Comforter will not come unto you; but if I depart, I will send him unto you." It is also likely that the words of Christ, "Blessed are they that mourn: for they shall be comforted " (Mt. 5:4) may have had a Messianic connotation.

Godly men like Simeon undoubtedly did mourn, seeing the reign of wickedness and sin. They were to be comforted by the coming of the Messiah, the consolation of Israel. There were others in Israel who were waiting for this consolation. These were the righteous and devout. We see them in the Gospel of Luke in the persons of Elisabeth, Zacharias, Simeon, and Anna the prophetess, who "looked for redemption in Jerusalem" (Lk. 2:38). These waited for the Messiah longingly, prayerfully, patiently.

Naturally, the consolation of Israel took on a different meaning with different people, varying according to their spiritual understanding and insight. To some, the consolation meant the cessation of foreign oppression and deliverance from Roman rule, the punishment of the ungodly of Israel, and above all the restoration of Israel's earthly kingdom in all its ancient glory as under the great kings, David and Solomon. We hear echoes of this intense longing in the question of the disciples, recorded in Acts 1:6, "When they therefore were come together, they asked of him, saying, Lord, wilt thou at this time restore again the kingdom to Israel?"

The Dead Sea Scrolls help us to learn a little more about the Messianic expectation, which certain groups of Jewish people nurtured about the time between the two eras.[2]

Certain devout circles in Israel like those of the community of

Qumran waited for the consolation of Israel to appear through the birth of a divine, superhuman personality in fulfillment of the great Isaianic prophecy (Isa. 7:14; 9:1; 9:6).[3]

Some sought to hasten the day of the consolation of Israel by revolts and by violence (Mt. 11:12) against the foreign oppressors. One of these Zealots was Judas of Galilee (Acts 5:37). Many others are mentioned in the works of Josephus.

There were also those who, like Simeon and Anna the prophetess, waited patiently for His coming, praying and fasting. For them, the Messiah's mission was of a spiritual nature. Their consolation was more in keeping with the prophetic vision of Isaiah 53, Psalm 22, and other Messianic prophecies.

Miriam, the virgin of Nazareth, was undoubtedly among those who, like Simeon, waited for the consolation of Israel and, like Anna, "looked for the redemption."

CHAPTER TWELVE

Between Boyhood and Manhood

The evangelist Matthew in the second chapter of his Gospel relates some of the miraculous events which attended the infancy of Jesus. We hear of "wise men from the east" who followed the star looking for the King of the Jews. We read about their encounter with crafty old Herod. We follow them as they pay homage to the infant Savior in Bethlehem. We learn about the flight of the holy family into Egypt and of Herod's cruel murder of the innocents and the return to Nazareth after Herod's death.

Israel's fervent hope for a divine deliverer was undoubtedly known among the learned men of the East and West. We know that during that period many spiritually-minded Gentiles (Virgil for instance) were influenced by Israel's vision. In their own way they too looked for a deliverer from the bondage of evil under which the human race was groaning.

The visit of the wise men from the east and their homage to the King of the Jews was, as it were, a prophetic event projecting the times when the Hope of Israel as envisioned in Genesis 49:10 and Isaiah 55:5 would become a reality:

> *The sceptre shall not depart from Judah, nor a lawgiver from between his feet, until Shiloh come; and unto him shall the gathering of the people be.*

> *Behold, thou shalt call a nation that thou knowest not, and nations that knew not thee shall run unto thee because of the LORD thy God, and for the Holy One of Israel; for he that glorified thee.*

Just as an overture "predicts" the main theme of a great symphony, so did the wise men, representative of the Gentile world, who followed the star of Bethlehem, anticipate the time when many from among the nations shall pay homage to the King of the Jews.

"I shall see him, but not now: I shall behold him, but not nigh; there shall come a Star out of Jacob, and a Sceptre shall rise out of Israel" (Num. 24:17).

Again and again Matthew emphasizes the parallel between the plight of the infant Jesus and the infancy of historic Israel.

And was there until the death of Herod; that it might be fulfilled which was spoken of the Lord by the prophet, saying, Out of Egypt have I called my son.

In Rama was there a voice heard, lamentation, and weeping, and great mourning, Rachel weeping for her children, and would not be comforted, because they are not. And he came and dwelt in a city called Nazareth: that it might be fulfilled which was spoken by the prophets, He shall be called a Nazarene (Mt. 2:15, 18, 23).

It should be remembered that in the Jewish mind the Messiah was the representative Israelite, indeed the personification of Israel. The rabbis maintained that "Israel and her Messiah are one."

From time immemorial Egypt has been the refuge of Israelites who, for one reason or another were in trouble. (Abraham, Jacob, and his sons; later, Jeroboam, Jeremiah, and others). At the turn of the era there was a very large and influential Jewish community in Egypt. Most of them settled in Alexandria, where they even had their own temple which rivaled in splendor the one in Jerusalem. It was thither that the Angel of the Lord directed Joseph and his family to find refuge from the murderous cruelty and mad jealousy of Herod the Great.

After the death of Herod (which, as we have already mentioned, occurred on March 12, 4 BC)[1], they returned to Nazareth. By this time the child Jesus may have been about a year or perhaps two years old. Matthew 3 takes up this story of Jesus. We see Him already grown to mature manhood as He comes down from Galilee to the river Jordan to be baptized by John (v. 13).

The other Gospels (with the exception of the Temple incident in Luke 2) also introduce Jesus at the point when He is about to begin His ministry.

THE SILENT YEARS

Between Matthew 2 and 3, a period of about 30 years of silence has passed in the life of Jesus. What happened during that time? What did He do during these years which constituted about nine-tenths of His earthly life? With whom did He associate? Did the boy Jesus go to school? Who were His teachers? What were the influences which contributed to His growth "in grace and wisdom"? (Lk. 2:40).

These are some of the questions which generations of His followers have been asking, without finding a satisfactory answer. These years have come to be known as the hidden or silent years.

Only one brief gleam of light bursts upon our complete ignorance of the events in the life of Jesus before He entered upon His ministry as Messiah and King of Israel, a ministry which led to His coronation with a crown of thorns and to a cross. This brief incident in the life of the boy Jesus is recorded in Luke 2:41–52.

THE INFANCY GOSPELS

The so-called Infancy Gospels of the second to fourth centuries AD, provide us with little reliable information concerning these years. These "Gospels" are apparently the result of the natural yearning of the early Christians to fill out the painful gap of the almost unbearable ignorance concerning the childhood of Jesus. Vivid imaginations and the free flight of fancy made up for that which history did not provide.

The infancy stories preserved in the non-canonical or apocryphal Gospels are sometimes amusing, occasionally bizarre, and often blasphemous. They attribute to Jesus thoughts, actions, and sentiments which are totally unworthy of our divine Savior, but which however, reflect the popular thinking of some early Christians. Here are some of the infancy legends as related in the so-called Gospel of Thomas (preserved in Greek and Latin manuscripts of the fifth and sixth centuries):

I, Thomas the Israelite, tell unto you, even all the brethren that are of the Gentiles, to make known unto you the works of the childhood

*of our Lord Jesus Christ and his mighty deeds, even all that he did
when he was born in our land: whereof the beginning is thus:*

*This little child Jesus when he was five years old was playing at the
ford of a brook: and he gathered together the waters that flowed
there into pools, and made them straightway clean, and commanded them by his word alone. And having made soft clay, he
fashioned thereof twelve sparrows. And there were also many other
little children playing with him.*

*And a certain Jew when he saw what Jesus did, playing upon the
sabbath day, departed straightway and told his father Joseph: Lo,
thy child is at the brook, and he hath taken clay and fashioned
twelve little birds, and hath polluted the sabbath day. And Joseph
came to the place and saw: and cried out to him, saying: Wherefore
doest thou these things on the sabbath, which it is not lawful to do?
But Jesus clapped his hands together and cried out to the sparrows
and said to them: Go! and the sparrows took their flight and went
away chirping. And when the Jews saw it they were amazed, and
departed and told their chief men that which they had seen Jesus
do.*[2]

As an example of legends which attribute to the child Jesus unworthy
sentiments, we quote again from the same Gospel of Thomas:

*But the son of Annas the scribe was standing there with Joseph;
and he took a branch of a willow and dispersed the waters which
Jesus had gathered together. And when Jesus saw what was done,
he was wroth and said unto him: O evil, ungodly, and foolish one,
what hurt did the pools and the waters do thee? behold, now also
thou shalt be withered like a tree, and shalt not bear leaves, neither
root, nor fruit. And straightway that lad withered up wholly, but
Jesus departed and went unto Joseph's house. But the parents of him
that was withered took him up, bewailing his youth, and brought
him to Joseph, and accused him 'for that thou has such a child which
doeth such deeds.'*

After that again he went through the village, and a child ran and dashed against his shoulder. And Jesus was provoked and said unto him: Thou shalt not finish thy course (lit. go all thy way). And immediately he fell down and died. But certain when they saw what was done said: Whence was this young child born, for that every word of his is an accomplished work? and the parents of him that was dead came unto Joseph, and blamed him, saying: Thou that has such a child canst not dwell with us in the village: or do thou teach him to bless and not to curse: for he slayeth our children.[3]

THE BOY JESUS IN THE TEMPLE

For a brief moment the veil of obscurity is lifted as we watch the boy Jesus and His parents come to Jerusalem for the Passover feast. This incident, like a flash of lightning in the darkness of night, affords us a glimpse of teenage Jesus. Here we also gain some insight into His relationship to Miriam and Joseph.

It has been suggested by some that the occasion of the visit of the boy Jesus was His *bar mitzvah*. Traditionally, a Jewish boy becomes at the age of 13, "a son of the commandment"; that is, he becomes a responsible member of the religious community.

However, this view can hardly be correct. Jesus was only 12, and Luke 2:41–52, makes it quite clear that the occasion was the Feast of the Passover, when the parents of Jesus, in accordance with the Law of Moses, went up to celebrate the Feast of Passover, one of the three pilgrim feasts (Ex. 23:14, 17). It may be that this was the first time that Jesus, being 12 years of age, was considered old enough to make the fairly strenuous pilgrimage to Jerusalem. Perhaps His participation in this pilgrimage and in the temple service was considered an introduction to His religious coming of age.

Josephus may have exaggerated when he said that during the pilgrim holidays there were about 3 million people in Jerusalem, while normally there were only about 120,000 inhabitants.

The visit to Jerusalem and to the Temple, the view of the joyful celebrating masses, must have made a profound impression on the mind of the extremely intelligent and sensitive boy. A boy of 12 is naturally inquisitive; he wants to see, hear, and learn everything. It must be remembered that the turn of the era was the age of two great pillars of traditional Judaism, of Hillel the Elder and of Shammai, his great rival. The school of Hillel, the more gentle interpreter of Jewish lore, and the school of Shammai, of much sterner disposition, contended for primacy over the minds of the Jewish people. The followers of these luminaries of early Judaism contended with one another also within the precincts of the Temple. Keen and incisive questions were asked by the best minds in Israel. Answers were given by doctors of the Law of Moses which later became the definitive rules of the Jews (the *Halachah*) as preserved in the Talmud.

The boy Jesus, endowed with a God-given wisdom, had the opportunity to ask some questions which went to the very heart of man's relationship to God and Israel's redemption. Already then the boy Jesus drew to Himself the attention of the spiritual giants in Israel.

However, our primary concern in this Temple incident is to learn what was the relationship between the boy Jesus and His parents, especially with Miriam. Only Jesus is mentioned as being in the company of His parents on the pilgrimage to Jerusalem. His brothers and, sisters are not mentioned. Does this prove that Jesus was an only child? Not at all. Since Jesus was the firstborn and only 12 years old at the time, obviously his brothers and sisters would be much too young to participate in the long pilgrimage from Nazareth to Jerusalem. However, the question of His brothers and sisters will be discussed later.

We can well imagine that, among the hundreds of thousands of pilgrims who thronged to Jerusalem, it was easy for the child Jesus to vanish from the sight of His parents without them becoming unduly alarmed. There would be many friends and acquaintances who were making the sacred and joyful pilgrimage in company, grouped together according to the towns and villages from which they came. How easy for a lovable 12-year-old to become detained by friends or relatives. Miriam and Joseph naturally assumed that He was visiting with His kinsfolk or friends, when in reality He was "sitting in the midst of the doctors, both hearing them, and asking them questions" (Lk. 2:46).

"Son, why hast thou thus dealt with us? behold, thy father and I have sought thee sorrowing" (v. 48). These were the first words of reproach which the frantic mother said to her missing boy. How natural and understandable were these words. It is interesting to note that

Miriam addressed Jesus as "Son." Yet we never hear Jesus call Miriam "Mother." This significant fact must also be discussed later. We notice that referring to Joseph, Miriam calls him "thy father." How much did Jesus know, at this stage in His life, about His supernatural origin? This we do not know. What did Miriam tell the child Jesus concerning the circumstances of His birth? It would be presumptuous to try to fathom these things. Undoubtedly as He grew older He became aware of His supernatural origin. However, for all practical purposes of daily life and communication, and as far as the people of Nazareth were concerned, Miriam was His mother and Joseph His father.

The incident in the Temple indicated that already at this stage in His life, Jesus was aware of His extraordinary position. In answer to Miriam's remark, "thy father and I have sought thee sorrowing," came the pointed rejoinder, "Wist ye not that I must be about my Father's business?" (v. 49).

Already then the boy Jesus was making it clear that the relationship to his "father" Joseph and to His mother Miriam must be subordinated to a relationship of a higher order and to a task so exalted and holy that it was beyond their ken. Already then He was making it clear to Miriam and Joseph that He came into the world to do His Father's business. From then on we shall hear Jesus give answers which went far beyond the scope of the original question.

There was something totally and utterly different between the relationship of the child Jesus to His parents and the relationship of other Jewish children to their parents.

One of the most emphasized commandments taught, observed, and inculcated in every Jewish child was, "Honor thy father and mother." The Talmud is full of stories to what length the great rabbis and outstanding men of Israel went in their efforts to observe this commandment. We recall His rebuke to those unworthy sons who sought to evade their filial obligations to honor their parents by the subterfuge of invoking a *Corban* (something which is dedicated only to God, Mk. 7:11).

We can be sure that in no way would the holy child Jesus, so steeped in the Law of Moses and in the teachings of His people, transgress against the fourth commandment, "Honor thy father and thy mother." And yet, in spite of all this, there was an ever-increasing sense of estrangement, of "otherness," gradually developing between Jesus and His parents, as

He grew older and the days of His public ministry were approaching.

He was essentially of heaven, whereas Miriam and Joseph, for all their devout and godly lives, were still children of a totally different dispensation. Surpassing the obligation to His mother and foster father was the express task of Jesus to honor and to glorify His heavenly Father. This task must take precedence over any other consideration and the most tender human ties. To misunderstand this foundational truth is to misunderstand the very essence of His life. The whole New Testament with amazing foreknowledge of subsequent history repeatedly seeks to warn against and to forestall the error of Mariolatry, the undue or excessive veneration and worship of the mother of Jesus.

The incident in the Temple, and the brief exchange between mother and son presaged a turning point in the life of Jesus. At the age of 12, Jesus for the first time asserted His divine mission. Although He went back to Nazareth in perfect harmony and in submission to His parents, Miriam already had started to learn the lesson of every disciple, that "He must increase and I must decrease" (Jn. 3:30). How difficult and painful this lesson was for Miriam and Joseph is indicated by the evangelist: "And they understood not the saying which he spake unto them" (Lk. 2:50).

If we may be permitted to use a simile, the Temple incident was the point when the fledgling eagle for the first time had spread His wings, and before the amazed and disturbed eyes of His parents, soared up high, beyond their horizon.

Introspective Miriam, inclined to a life of meditation and contemplation, "kept all these sayings in her heart" (v. 51).

THREE FOUNTAINS

During those silent years Jesus probably learned all that devout Jewish parents and the teachers in the synagogue and community school of Nazareth could teach Him, and much more beside.

Three main fountains of wisdom were available to the boy and the young man Jesus in those silent years.

The first was the direct and mystical communion between Jesus and His heavenly Father. It probably was exercised in the periods of prayer and intensive meditation to which Jesus was apparently accustomed from His earliest days. What transpired there is beyond the ken of any man. This is holy ground which no man dare trespass.

The second foundation of wisdom was the one which He learned at the knees of His godly Jewish parents. All life's activities, from morning to night, from cradle to grave, were hallowed by the devout customs and rites observed in His parents' home and among His people. In the synagogue He often heard the Bible read in Hebrew and interpreted in the vernacular Aramaic. He no doubt knew by heart all the prayers customary among His people. The hopes, the fears, the songs, and the yearnings of oppressed Israel were familiar to Him from the earliest days of His life. He knew intimately the daily life around Him.

Sometimes He must have watched the ways of the farmer at sowing and during the harvest season. The shouting of the sellers and the haggling of the buyers in the Nazareth *shuk* (market place) must have been familiar sounds to Him. He saw the heavy-burdened toilers and laborers in the narrow streets producing their wares for the small town and surrounding villages. Often, perhaps daily, He attended the little synagogue of Nazareth, where He heard and took part in the community prayers. The synagogue most probably also doubled for a public school where Jesus learned His *Alef Beth* (ABCs). Soon the gifted student was promoted to the reading of the Torah. He watched the Pharisees and the learned men expound the Scriptures with solemnity and sometimes with great pride in their learning. He observed the wealthy but often despised publicans. Perhaps He sometimes visited the widowed neighbor who lost a precious coin and turned the house upside down until she found it. He took part in the games of the children and was always a good, though sometimes very serious companion. All these experiences were later reflected in His parables and sayings.

Then there were the lush, beautiful, green smiling fields and terraced hills of Galilee, full of vineyards and olive groves. Here and there singing and playing shepherds would tend their flocks or herds.

Sometimes He would sit down on one of the numerous hills around Nazareth from where He could catch a glimpse of the Sea of Galilee or the distant Great Sea (the Mediterranean), of glimmering white snow-covered Mount Hermon to the north and of the multi-colored carpet of the verdant, lovely valley of Esdraelon below.

In the spring, the hills would be ablaze with red, yellow, blue, and purple flowers, anemones, lilies of the valley, wild roses, blossoming shrubs and fruit trees, all of it the handiwork of his own Father. From all these fountains and much that is beyond our comprehension Jesus drank. And as He drank from the eternal fountains, "the child grew and waxed strong in spirit, filled with wisdom and the grace of God was upon him" (Lk. 2:40).

When He grew older and stronger, He went about helping Joseph in his carpenter shop. He became a carpenter Himself (Mk. 6:3), no doubt a good one at that.

These were years of physical and spiritual growth, of treasuring up in His soul the ancient heritage of Israel, the beauty of nature in lovely Galilee, years of listening in to the voice of His Father in heaven and absorbing His unfathomable wisdom and boundless love.

One day this wisdom and love would pour out of His heart and flood the world with a tidal wave of grace. But for the time being, "Jesus increased in wisdom and stature, and in favor with God and man" (Lk. 2:52).

CHAPTER THIRTEEN

The Wedding in Cana

And the third day there was a marriage in Cana of Galilee; and the mother of Jesus was there: And both Jesus was called, and his disciples, to the marriage (Jn. 2:1–2).

Some 18 years have passed since we last saw Jesus as a 12-year-old boy in the Temple in Jerusalem. Eighteen years is a long time in the life of any young man. The boy Jesus had in the meantime grown and matured into full manhood, and was now about 30 years old (Lk. 3:23). Now the appointed time had come for His public ministry.

In token of submission, He allowed Himself to be baptized by John the Baptist and was proclaimed by him as "the lamb of God which taketh away the sin of the world" (Jn. 1:29) and "whose shoes I am not worthy to bear" (Mt. 3:11). Soon after, Jesus called His first disciples in Galilee. Among these was a certain man called Nathanael, a native of Cana (Jn.1:45–51).

It may be that this new contact with Nathanael resulted in an invitation extended to the young rabbi, His mother, and His disciples to come to the wedding in Cana of Galilee. Always sociable and gladly mingling with people, Jesus accepted the invitation and came accompanied by His mother and His followers.

It is interesting to note that in this particular instance, Joseph is conspicuous by his absence, and is never mentioned again in the Gospels, except once, as the presumed father of Jesus (6:42). It is quite likely that some time between the incident in the Temple described in Luke 2 and the entry of Jesus upon His public ministry, Joseph had died. How old was Joseph when he died? We do not know. Extra-canonical writings are contradictory and confusing, as usual. Assuming that Joseph married

Miriam at the normal marrying age for Jewish young men, which was about 18, and that he died before the beginning of the public ministry of Jesus, Joseph's span of life was probably between 40-50 years. This was better than average for hard-working and toiling folks of that era.

Wedding feasts among the Jews traditionally lasted seven days. The near relatives and close friends stayed for the whole period of festivities. It was customary then, as it is today, for the father of the bride to foot the bill. "The Governor of the feast," who was appointed by the parents of the bride, was in charge of the wedding arrangements and the details of the feast. To run out of wine, so essential to the wedding festivities, was a most embarrassing situation.

"And when they wanted wine, the mother of Jesus saith unto him, They have no wine" (Jn. 2:3).

This was an indirect request that Jesus do something about it, also an implied expression of Miriam's faith that Jesus could produce the wine, if He so wished.

Was there any other motivation behind Miriam's request? This is quite possible. Conscious of the fact that Jesus was born of the Holy Spirit, she knew that He came into the world as the Redeemer of Israel. Now He was about 30 years old. Was it not high time that He should publicly manifest His divine power, and thus establish His position as Messiah of Israel?

Perhaps there was in her request also an unconscious element of maternal pride and ambition. If she could only induce Him now to demonstrate His miraculous powers, this would commit Him to launch out upon His Messianic career, for which she was so anxiously waiting, and perhaps at the same time dreading.

"WOMAN, WHAT HAVE I TO DO WITH THEE?"

The reaction of Jesus to His mother's request was quite startling, both in form and substance: "Jesus saith unto her, Woman, what have I to do with thee? Mine hour is not yet come" (v. 4).

The most casual reader of this incident must consider it strange that Jesus should address His mother as "Woman." It sounds harsh and unnatural. We would expect Jesus to address her as "Mother." For a son to address his mother "Woman" was most unusual then, as it would be today.

When Bathsheba, the mother of King Solomon, came to him to plead for her son, Adonijah, the king's half-brother, Solomon received his mother with the greatest courtesy and addressed her in this manner:

"Ask on, my mother: for I will not say thee nay" (1 Ki. 2:20), although Solomon did refuse his mother's request, and Adonijah was put to death.

The point is, that the natural and courteous way would be for Jesus to call Miriam, *Imma* which means "mother," and not *Ita* (woman). And yet, nowhere is it recorded in the Gospels that He ever publicly called Miriam "Mother."

Catholic exegetes always maintain that the word *woman* has an honorific connotation, that it is as if He called her "Lady."[1] But this assertion is unsubstantiated by any usage in contemporary literature. Neither in the New Testament, nor in the Apocrypha, nor in the Talmudic literature which is nearest to that time, do we find anywhere such usage. The appellation *woman* indicates a somber and matter-of-fact relationship between Jesus and His mother, a relationship which emphasizes distance rather than closeness.

To the Syrophenician woman He said: "O woman, great is thy faith" (Mt. 15:28). In the same manner Jesus addressed Himself to the Samaritan woman: "Woman, believe me, the hour cometh, when ye shall neither in this mountain, nor yet at Jerusalem, worship the Father" (Jn. 4:21).

In the same way He addresses Himself to the woman caught in adultery: "Woman, where are those thine accusers?" (8:10).

While hanging on the cross He entrusted His mother to the beloved disciple with the words: "Woman, behold thy son!" (19:26). Again, the risen Jesus addresses Himself with these tender words to Miriam of Magdala (Mary Magdalene), "Woman, why weepest thou?" (20: 15).

Consistently He used this form of address when speaking to any woman. And Miriam was no exception. Only on two occasions did Jesus address Himself to a woman, calling her by her name: "Martha, Martha" (Lk. 10:41), and after the resurrection, "Mary" (Jn. 20:16).

Jewish custom imposed upon men a certain rigid and austere manner of dealing with womenfolk. Men generally kept to themselves. It should not be imagined that at the wedding at Cana the women mingled freely with the men or sat together at the banquet table. This would constitute a breach of Jewish etiquette. The women probably sat together with the bride or helped at the tables while the men sat with the bridegroom. For Miriam to come from the women's quarter to inform Jesus that "they have no wine," was in itself a breach of etiquette and a liberty on her part based on assumed maternal privilege.

In calling His mother "Woman," Jesus did not intend this as a discourtesy but rather as a mild rebuke. It was important that He draw clearly and definitely the demarcation line between Himself and His mother or any person who on the basis of physical kinship would claim special privilege or priority. To do otherwise would contradict everything He taught, exemplified or came to accomplish.

His form of address, "Woman," serves to emphasize the basic "otherness" of Jesus. While He was a child under the tutelage of His parents, He was subject to them. But now their relationship must be on a different plane. Earthly ties, however close and tender, must not infringe on His redemptive mission.

We find this attitude expressed not only in His own personal relationship to His mother, but in His teaching of others. Speaking to His disciples about the price of following Him, He said:

He that loveth father or mother more than me is not worthy of me; and he that loveth son or daughter more than me is not worthy of me; and he that taketh not his cross, and followeth after me, is not worthy of me" (Mt. 10:37–38).

Family ties and loyalties, important and precious as they may be, must become subservient to a higher loyalty. He who demanded of others willingness to forsake father and mother in order to follow Him, could set no lesser standard for Himself.[2]

The de-emphasizing of physical relationship in favor of a higher relationship is again brought out in the story of the visit of Miriam and His brethren:

Then came to him his mother and his brethren, and could not come to him for the press. And it was told him by certain which said, Thy mother and thy brethren stand without, desiring to see thee. And He answered and said unto them, My mother and my brethren are these which hear the word of God, and do it. (Lk. 8:19–21)

His characteristic answer again emphasizes not physical kinship, but kinship of a higher order.

Those who would attribute to Miriam a special position, by virtue of her being the mother of Jesus, point to the fact that Miriam did hear the word of God and believed, that she did do what God commanded her. This is so.

Yet the fact that Jesus puts "my mother" in juxtaposition with "my brethren" who, we are informed, did not believe in Him as yet (Jn. 7:3–5) points up the fact that Jesus claimed as His true family all "who hear His voice and do it." This included Miriam as a member of this universal family who belong to Him, but only as a disciple and a follower. Any claim to kinship with Jesus must be one of faith and not of flesh. The incident recorded in Luke 11:27–28 further reinforces and emphasizes the same truth.

The whole tenor of all the Gospel narratives clearly points to the fact that Miriam's was not the exalted position of "the Mother of God" of later Mariology or Mariolatry, to whom her son Jesus owed obedience and allegiance, but rather that her position was that of a humble disciple to her Master, of a redeemed sinner to her Savior. True, He was her son and this honor no one can take away from her, but He was much more than Miriam's son. Above all, He was her Lord and Savior. Physical descent was always subordinated in His thinking to the fact that He was the Son of God. On one occasion Jesus asked the Pharisees:

> *What think ye of Christ? Whose son is he? They say unto him, The son of David. He saith unto them. How then doth David in spirit call him Lord, saying, the LORD said unto my Lord, sit thou on my right hand, till I make thine enemies thy footstool? If David then call him Lord, how is he his son?* (Mt. 22:42–45).

That Jesus was the Son of David was indeed important, but far more important was the truth that He was David's Lord. Miriam had to learn this truth, and so must we. So much for the form of appellation "Woman."

"WHAT HAVE I TO DO W1TH THEE?"

We must now turn from the unusual form of address to the meaning of His striking reply to Miriam.

"Woman, what have I to do with thee?" is an expression of dissent. It implies rebuke. It means, "What do we have in common, you and I?" What Jesus actually said to Miriam was perhaps a gentle but clear rebuke of her impatience and interference with His plans. "Mine hour is not yet come." He could not be rushed. Henceforth, Jesus must go at His own pace and do the will of His Father in His own way and in His own time. He could not be guided by Miriam, but rather by the wisdom from above which was so peculiarly His own. Not the will of Miriam but the will of His Father in heaven would henceforth determine His life and His work.

Human motives, however noble and well-meaning, must not sway Him in His God-appointed mission, nor interfere with the course of its fulfillment.

Yet, Miriam's essential humility and submission to the will of God becomes again evident in her words to the servants, "Whatsoever he saith unto you, do it" (Jn. 2:5). This was the glory of Miriam, that she was willing to submerge her own natural inclinations in His will. She understood that what really mattered was what Jesus commanded, that in the final analysis, obedience was due not to her, but to Him. Instruction and the word of command must come from Jesus and not from His mother. The fulfillment of our petitions is vested in Jesus and not in Miriam, whom God in His unfathomable grace and wisdom chose to be His mother.

That Jesus did nevertheless perform the expected miracle of turning the water into wine was apparently out of consideration for the embarrassed host and in order not to further embarrass Miriam. Not to accede to her request would have been against the graciousness of His whole character as well as against all Jewish family tradition, which strongly emphasized parental honor. There is also this consideration: According to ancient tradition, in the days of the Messiah wine would be as plentiful as water. If Jesus were to turn water into wine, this would further confirm His Messianic character. In all probability Miriam was well aware of this tradition, and so were His disciples, as we read:

"This beginning of miracles (the Greek word is "signs"—*toon semeioon*) did Jesus in Cana of Galilee and manifested forth his glory; and his disciples believed on him" (2:11).

This miracle was a sign, a portent of things to come, a token of His Messianic power and dignity.

Miriam's faith in His ability to do the seemingly impossible may also have had something to do with the final granting of her request.

We recall a similar situation when Jesus was touched by the faith of the Syrophenician woman to whom He granted her request after apparently having refused her at first.

"Then Jesus answered and said unto her, O woman, great is thy faith: be it unto thee even as thou wilt. And her daughter was made whole from that very hour" (Mt. 15:28).

The saying of Jesus, "Woman, what have I to do with thee?" was meant to be a word to the wise, which was not lost on the sensitive and contemplative soul of His mother. At the wedding of Cana, Miriam was made to learn gently but firmly, that she was not to presume on her physical kinship to Jesus but, like any other of His followers, must submit to His will. There were painful lessons which Miriam had to learn but their sum total spelled out experience-by-experience and letter-by-letter that Jesus was LORD and SAVIOR.

CHAPTER FOURTEEN

"The Brethren" of Jesus

Is not this the carpenter's son? is not his mother called Mary? and his brethren, James, and Joses, and Simon, and Judas? and his sisters, are they not all with us? Whence hath this man all these things? (Mt. 13:55–56).

One of the most difficult and controversial issues in the study of Miriam is the question: Were the persons mentioned in Matthew 13:55–56 and Mark 6:3 as "brethren and sisters" of Jesus actually His brothers and sisters, or were they cousins or other kinsmen?

On the answer to this question the whole structure of Roman Catholic Mariology hinges.

Here again we can only rely on the New Testament as the sole dependable source of our information. What then does the New Testament have to say about this matter?

We shall proceed on the sound principle of scriptural exegesis which says that "if the natural sense makes good sense, seek no other sense."

In the Gospel of Matthew we read that on the occasion when Jesus was teaching in the synagogue in His own country (Galilee), the people were amazed at His wisdom and mighty works, and they said, "Is not this the carpenter's son? Is not his mother called Mary? and his brethren, James and Joses, and Simon, and Judas? and his sisters, are they not all with us?" (Mt. 13:55–56).

A parallel passage is found in Mark 6:3, with the difference that there Jesus is referred to not as "the carpenter's son" but as "the carpenter." Both statements are easily reconcilable since He was both the carpenter's son as well as being a carpenter Himself, before entering upon His public ministry. Trades and occupations usually ran in the family. The names of the brothers recorded in the two Gospels are the same. In the absence of any other explanatory or qualifying statements, the natural and obvious meaning of the words "brothers" and "sisters" is plain. Why the persistent attempt by some to read into the Gospel record a different sense than the obvious?

From early times, the opinion spread among Christians of Gentile origin and pagan background, that the mother of Jesus was always a virgin (*Semper Virgo*), before the birth of Jesus and after. Behind this belief was the widespread idea, common to many Mediterranean cults, that virginity and celibacy were intrinsically a state superior to that of marriage.

Among the Greeks there was a cult of Hestia, the eternally virgin goddess of the Olympus, who was worshiped as the deity of the domestic hearth. Later Hestia merged with the cults of Cybele and Demeter, the Universal Mother.

In Rome Hestia was known as Vesta, and her priestesses were called Vestal Virgins. The senior priestess of the Vestal cult was known as the Virgo Maxima—the Great Virgin.

Of course such cults were entirely alien to scriptural thinking. Marriage among the Jews was considered a sacred institution established by God Himself. The bearing of children was a religious and sacred obligation, and childlessness was looked upon as a grievous condition, practically a disaster, which in the eyes of the rabbis justified divorce.

Yet the vow of virginity, both among men and women, was not altogether unknown among the Jews. As an example, the daughter of Jephthah might be mentioned (Jud. 11:37–39). Celibacy was occasionally practiced among some Nazarites and also among some of the Essenes, an ascetic sect. But these were exceptions. Celibacy as such was never upheld in the Old Testament as an ideal, rather the contrary was true.

What then are the arguments against considering the brethren and sisters as the literal and physical brothers and sisters of Jesus and children of His mother, Miriam? A number of arguments have been advanced by those who are opposed to the obvious and literal sense of the words *brother* and *sister*.

THE LINGUISTIC ARGUMENT

Some maintain that the word *brethren* (Greek *adelfoi*), in our text, does not necessarily indicate a physical brother but may mean a cousin, a relative or even a fellow member of the community. It has been pointed out, for example, that Abraham called his nephew Lot a brother. "Let there be no strife, I pray thee, between me and thee, and between my herdmen and thy herdmen, for we be brethren" [Hebrew, *ahim*] (Gen. 13:8).

Actually, Lot was Abraham's nephew, his brother's son (11:31). It is true that the Hebrew term *brother* can be used, as in the English language, in a wider sense than the strict meaning of the word. But where *brother* or *brethren* in the Old Testament is used in a more general sense, the context leaves us in no doubt about this. But is it conceivable that the inspired authors of the New Testament, the evangelists Matthew and Mark, would leave us in uncertainty about a fact so basic to our faith, as the Church of Rome would have us believe this to be, without proper explanation? Would they use misleading language on so vital a point? Surely the evangelist Luke, the careful historian, who more than anyone else informed us about the mother of Jesus, would he not have had a definite word to say about so crucial a matter?

In the case of Abraham and Lot, Scripture makes it clear that Lot was a nephew and not a brother (Gen. 11:31). In the case of the brethren and sisters of Jesus, this is not so. Therefore, unless it can be proven otherwise, the natural and obvious meaning must stand.

THE "COUSINS" THEORY

Connected with what we called the linguistic argument is another line of argumentation which, for lack of a more suitable term, we have called the "cousins" theory.

In the 4th century, Jerome, the famous translator of the Vulgate, supported the theory that "the brethren" were actually the cousins of Jesus. This is inferred from John 19:25: "Now there stood by the cross of Jesus his mother, and his mother's sister, Mary the wife of Cleophas, and Mary Magdalene."

From the above text it is argued that Mary or Miriam, the wife of Cleophas or Alphaeus was the sister of Miriam, the mother of Jesus. But does this text support such a construction? It seems that four women are mentioned here and not three: 1, Mary, the mother of Jesus; 2, an unnamed sister of Mary; 3, Mary the wife of Cleophas; and 4, Mary

Magdalene.

Jerome and others have assumed that "Mary the wife of Cleophas" is just a gloss explaining "his mother's sister." If we accept the theory of Jerome, we must further assume that there were two sisters, both of them named Miriam or Mary. This is a most unlikely assumption, without a parallel in Jewish history.

We would further have to assume on the basis of Mark 15:40 ("There were also women looking on afar off, among whom was Mary Magdalene, and Mary the mother of James the Less and of Joses, and Salome"), that James the Less, mentioned among the apostles in Matthew 10:2–4, was a brother of Jesus. But we know that the brethren of Jesus did not believe on Him (Jn. 7:5). In any case, the brethren of Jesus are always listed separately, apart from the apostles (2:12; Acts 1:12–14).

Against the cousins theory must also be considered the fact that the Greek New Testament does not use the common Greek word for cousin, which is *anepsios,* a term frequently used by Josephus, who was contemporary to the writers of the Gospels.

Mariologists also maintain that it was not necessary to state explicitly the exact meaning of the term "brethren" because during the time of the events described in the Gospels, everybody knew the nature of this kinship.

However, since the Gospels were obviously written not only for their own generation and for their immediate environment, but also for strangers and for future generations, it is unthinkable that the evangelists would not spell out exactly the meaning of the term *brothers* or *brethren.* This is especially true since so much would depend on this in later mariological controversies.

Other even more fanciful arguments have been advanced in an effort to bolster the dogma of the perpetual virginity of Mary. One of these arguments seeks support in the prophecy of Ezekiel 44:2: "Then said the LORD unto me: This gate shall be shut, it shall not be opened, and no man shall enter in by it; because the LORD the God of Israel, hath entered in by it, therefore it shall be shut."

With such a fanciful exegesis almost anything can be "proven," at will. Such "proofs" only prove the lack of valid proof.

"THE ARGUMENT OF PROPRIETY"

Another argument advanced by the defenders of the perpetual virginity of Mary is "the argument of propriety." According to this reasoning, it was proper that Miriam always remain a virgin, even as her son was always virgin; that Joseph would not presume to have conjugal relations with his wife after she bore a son by the Holy Spirit.

This argument, although containing a certain measure of plausibility must, in the absence of scriptural proof, be considered as highly speculative and suspect of pagan inspiration and tendencies.

THE "HALF BROTHERS" THEORY

Another theory almost as old as the cousins theory is that of the "half brothers." According to that opinion, supported by Origen, Joseph was a widower when he married Miriam, and was the father of six children by his former wife. This would make them half brothers and half sisters of Jesus.

This tradition is recorded in the apocryphal *History of Joseph the Carpenter*, an Egyptian document of the fourth or fifth century preserved in the Arabic language. There we are told, among other things, that "Joseph was of Bethlehem; he was a carpenter and married and had four sons, Judas, Jesitos (Arab, Justus), James, Simon, and two daughters, Lysia (Arab, Asia) and Lydia. His wife died leaving James still young."

This tradition is also of questionable value, and presents an attempt to glorify Joseph and his feast day, long celebrated in Egypt.

Such are some of the very slender "proofs" that the brethren mentioned on a number of occasions in the New Testament and consistently in the company of the mother of Jesus, were not His actual brothers but His cousins or half-brothers and half sisters.

Against these arguments is the plain and obvious meaning of the Gospel statements, "his brethren and his sisters." The statement in Matthew 1:25 is also suggestive and significant: "And (Joseph) knew her not till she had brought forth her firstborn son: and he called his name Jesus."

At the very least there seems to be here a tacit implication that Joseph did "know her" after she brought forth her firstborn.

There is also the additional fact that the brethren of Jesus are usually mentioned, in the Gospels, in juxtaposition with Miriam, the mother of Jesus (Mk. 3:31–35; Mt. 12:46–50; Lk. 8:19–21). This creates the very strong presupposition that they were Miriam's natural children and that, after the birth of her firstborn son, the mother of our Lord gave birth to sons and daughters, who were the brothers and sisters of Jesus.

Nevertheless, in one special sense these kinsmen of Jesus were His half brothers and half sisters, because Jesus was born of the Holy Spirit and of Miriam, His mother; whereas the others were born of Miriam and Joseph. In this unique sense of the word, they were the half brothers and half sisters of Jesus.

No doubt the fact that Jesus was born of the Holy Spirit and His brothers and sisters were born in the natural way, was the root of misunderstanding, of trouble and tensions among the children of Miriam, for: "That which is born of the flesh is flesh, and that which is born of the Spirit is spirit" (Jn. 3:6).

JESUS AND HIS BROTHERS

As far as we can discern, the relationship between Jesus and His brothers does not seem to have been a harmonious one. We have already discussed that memorable occasion when His brethren and His mother came calling for Him. This incident is recorded by all three synoptic evangelists (Mk. 3:31–35; Mt. 12:46–50; Lk. 8:19–21):

There came then his brethren and his mother, and standing without, sent unto him, calling him. And the multitude sat about him, and they said unto him, Behold thy mother and thy brethren without seek for thee.

And he answered them saying, Who is my mother, or my brethren? And he looked round about on them which sat about him, and said, Behold my mother and my brethren! For whosoever shall do the will of God, the same is my brother, and my sister, and mother (Mk. 3:31-35).

It is possible that His brothers were concerned about the growing hostility of the religious leaders to Jesus and so came to restrain Him. On this occasion Miriam was with them. We do not think that Miriam shared their attitude, but probably came along in order to have a conciliating effect. There may have been other occasions when Miriam had to stand between her firstborn son and her other children to shield Him from their instinctive jealousy and lack of comprehension of His unique position.

It was under these circumstances that Jesus said:

> *Who is my mother, or my brethren? And he looked round about on them which sat about him, and said, Behold my mother and my brethren! For whosoever shall do the will of God, the same is my brother, and my sister, and mother* (Mk. 3:33–35).

This clearly indicates that, in His eyes, what really matters is not physical kinship but faith in God and doing His will.

Significantly in Mark 3:21, we read this strange and disturbing statement: "And when his friends heard of it, they went out to lay hold on him, for they said, He is beside himself."

It is interesting to note that in the Greek text the words translated in the King James Version as *his friends* do not appear, but instead there is the phrase, *hoi par autou* which means "they who belong to him." This was probably a discreet way of describing His nearest kinsmen. Isaac Salkinson's Hebrew translation of the New Testament renders this passage with *b'nei mishpachto*—the members of His family. This is more consistent with the Greek text. The Peshitta translation correctly renders this passage "and his relatives heard of it, and went out to seize him, for they said, He has lost his mind."[2]

These near kinsman of our Lord simply thought that He was out of His mind. Were these members of his family His brothers? At least this is probable. It should be remembered that when the Synoptic Gospels were completed, approximately AD 50-70, the brothers of Jesus were possibly still alive and considered esteemed members and pillars of the early Christian community. Delicacy would therefore suggest that they should not be embarrassed by exact identification.

Again in John 7:1–10, we have the record of a striking verbal exchange between Jesus and His brethren, who suggested that He go up to Jerusalem in order that His disciples might see "the works that thou doest" and that the world might come to know of Him. This suggestion apparently was not made in good faith but rather in a taunting manner, because immediately following their request we read the words, "For neither did his brethren believe in him" (Jn. 7:5).

The answer Jesus gave His brothers sheds light on the opinion He had about them at that stage of their relationship: "The world cannot hate you, but me it hateth, because I testify of it, that the works thereof are evil" (Jn. 7:7).

We know what Jesus thought concerning "the world" in this particular context: "If the world hate you, ye know that it hated me before it hated you. If ye were of the world, the world would love his own; but because ye are not of the world, but I have chosen you out of the world, therefore the world hateth you" (15:18–19).

In the judgment of Jesus His brothers belonged, at this stage of their unbelief, to this world. In the light of this we find the words related in John 7:10 particularly revealing: "But when his brethren were gone up, then went he also up unto the feast, not openly, but as it were in secret."

Jesus seemingly did not altogether trust His brothers!

All this leads us to the strong feeling that the relationship between Jesus and His brothers was far from being happy or harmonious. There may have also been a certain amount of jealousy because of His fame and the special attention given to Him by Miriam and Joseph when he was still alive. Perhaps there were fears of dangerous consequences for the whole family because of His strange ways.

It is also possible that the brothers of Jesus felt that, since Miriam was now a widow, their eldest brother should have assumed the place and responsibilities of their departed father, Joseph, and should not have roamed the country as a traveling preacher. In any event, as in so many other families with numerous brothers and sisters, there were enough elements of potential conflict to cause serious tension. However, in the case of Miriam's family these elements were even more pronounced than elsewhere.

Finally, we must submit this thought for consideration: We know that in the Old Testament the brothers of Joseph were extremely jealous and hostile to him. This culminated in their betrayal of Joseph and his being sold by them into Egypt as a slave. However the story had a happy ending. The despised Joseph rose to the position of viceroy of Egypt, second only to Pharaoh. Finally, after many grueling experiences the sons of Jacob repented and became reconciled to their long-counted-for-dead brother Joseph (Gen. 37—45).

On the basis of what we already know from the Gospels concerning the brothers of Jesus and the striking parallels between Joseph and Jesus, is it too much to assume that the brothers of Jesus acted in a rather similar manner to the brothers of Joseph? Is it possible that only the fact of the resurrection, and the exaltation of the "second Joseph" at last brought about the forgiveness and reconciliation between these New Testament counterparts of the brothers of Joseph?

It seems to us that the rejection of Jesus by His own people had to be, in the divine Providence, preceded by a rejection on the part of those who were of His immediate family. If this is so, then the words of the psalmist take on a strange and poignant prophetic significance: "I am become a stranger unto my brethren, and an alien unto my mother's children" (Ps. 69:8).

In this context the words "my brethren" and "my mother's children" could hardly be more suggestive.

The words of John the evangelist may have struck home more closely than most of us realize, when he wrote: "He came unto his own and his own (family) received him not" (Jn. 1:11).

This tension within her family undoubtedly was a cloud which overshadowed the daily life of Miriam, and an added burden upon her soul. Perhaps out of deference to Miriam and to her sons, who later became staunch believers in the crucified and risen Jesus, the evangelists preferred not to be too specific about these things.

CHAPTER FIFTEEN

Miriam at the Cross

Now there stood by the cross of Jesus his mother, and his mother's sister, Mary the wife of Cleophas, and Mary Magdalene (Jn. 19:25).

Miriam, standing at the cross of her son, has been the favorite theme of countless poets, composers, painters, and theologians. It is a great and moving theme; a mother at the feet of her dying and well-loved son.

It has the majesty of all great suffering and sorrow. It evokes within us chords of deepest compassion. Miriam, beneath the cross of her beloved son, might cry with Jeremiah of old: "Is it nothing to you, all ye that pass by? Behold, and see if there be any sorrow like unto my sorrow, which is done unto me" (Lam. 1:12).

Here, apparently, was the end of the road for her beloved son, the son of God's promise. All that was precious to her was now irrevocably nailed to the cross. Her mother's heart must have been breaking and dying with His—His agony, her own agony. Nailed also to the cross was not only her precious son, but Israel's hope, the salvation and the consolation of Israel, for which she and countless others had lived and waited, hoped and prayed unceasingly.

Did she know that her son would after three days rise again from the dead; that He would ascend into heaven? On several occasions Jesus had alluded to this:

Therefore doth my Father love me, because I lay down my life, that I might take it again. No man taketh it from me, but I lay it down of myself. I have power to lay it down, and I have power to take it again. This commandment have I received of my Father (Jn. 10:17–18).

Or His statement, "Destroy this temple, and in three days I will raise it up" (2:19). Yet somehow this truth had not penetrated the consciousness of His disciples. When the moment of truth arrived, His mother and disciples were disconsolate and distressed. Though God had revealed to Miriam the mystery of the incarnation and granted her an intimation about the purpose of His coming by giving Him the name of Jesus ("for he shall save his people from their sins," Mt. 1:21), yet much remained obscure to her. She was not privy to all of God's counsel. Like the eyes of the other disciples, her eyes too were kept from seeing all of the truth and all of the grandeur of her son's mission.

It would have been humanly understandable if she, like Peter, had abhorred the thought of His death upon the cross (16:22, 23). It would have been natural if Miriam, like the two disciples on the road to Emmaus, had also felt deeply disappointed and frustrated: "But we hoped that it was he which should have redeemed Israel" (Lk. 24:21). Yet in later speculations, Catholic Mariologists have sought to picture Mary in the role of a high priest presenting her son as a sacrifice for the sins of the world, thus joining her grief to the death of Jesus, and making Mary an associate in the act of redemption.

However, concerning all this, Scripture is silent. Not one tear of Miriam's is marked; not one heartbreaking sigh or agonized cry is recorded. Not one word of her inner torment has been left for posterity to consider. It is as if the Holy Spirit would not suffer that the person of Miriam should in any way distract our attention from the central figure of the Gospel, the Man on the cross.

Miriam, beneath the cross, personifies countless mothers of all times, dying a thousand deaths with their loved ones. And yet, Miriam's sorrow was different from that of any other mother, because her son was different from any other son. With His death, Israel's hope seemed to have died also. This mood of despondency seems to have been expressed by the two disciples on the road to Emmaus: "But we hoped that it had been he which should have redeemed Israel" (Lk. 24:2l).

THE SEVEN HEBREW MARTYRS

Before considering further the scene of Miriam at the cross, let us for a moment digress and look at another mother, one who witnessed the martyrdom of her seven sons.

The story is recorded in the apocryphal book of 2 Maccabees of the second century BC. It is remotely reminiscent of our theme. There we read about the seven Hebrew boys who died as martyrs for their faith. Their nameless mother was present at the scene of torture. She encouraged her sons rather to die than to break God's law and defile themselves by eating swine's flesh, as commanded by Antiochus, the wicked king of Syria.

The books of the Maccabees are not recognized by the Jews, nor by the Protestants as part of the biblical canon, but are included in the Roman Catholic Bible.

While the seven young men were being tortured, their mother encouraged them in the following words:

I cannot tell you how ye came into my womb; for I neither gave you breath nor life, neither was it I that formed the members of every one of you; But doubtless the Creator of the world, who formed the generation of man, and found out the beginning of all things, will also of his own mercy give you breath and life again, as ye now regard not your own selves for his laws' sake (2 Macc. 7:22–23).

After her sixth boy was killed, touched by her steadfast faith, the king encouraged her to persuade the youngest son to save his life by obeying his command.

And when he had exhorted her with many words, she promised him that she would counsel her son. But she bowing herself toward him, laughing the cruel tyrant to scorn, spake in her country language on this manner: O my son, have pity upon me that bare thee nine months in my womb, and gave thee suck three years, and nourished thee, and brought thee up unto this age, and endured the troubles of education.

I beseech thee, my son, look upon the heaven and the earth, and all

that is therein, and consider that God made them of things that
were not; and so was mankind made likewise. Fear not this thy
mentor, but, being worthy of thy brethren, take thy death, that
I may receive thee again in mercy with thy brethren (2 Macc.
7:26–29)[1]

When they finally killed the seventh boy, the mother was also put
to death.

The book of 2 Maccabees was addressed to the Jewish community
in Egypt and apparently was written in order to encourage them to
hold fast to their faith and to preserve the unity of scattered Israel.

The second century before Christ was an age of terrible cruelty and
persecution of the Jews by the Hellenized kings of Syria who sought
to spread Greek civilization in their empire. No doubt many Jews died
for their faith, rather than submit to forced desecration of the law and
to assimilation.

The story of the seven young martyrs and their mother has all the
marks of pious fiction. They all behave like book heroes. Before they die
they each deliver their little oration of faith and defiance. The mother
in a similar manner behaves in the stylized way of a fictional heroine.
The early Christians cherished this story because it encouraged them
to endure their own martyrdom.

The contrast between this story and the Gospel scene of Miriam at
the cross is striking. Here there is a total absence of heroics and speeches,
only silent grief and agony, which had reached the point beyond words
or even lament. This is why Miriam at the cross is so deeply moving
and also credible.

THE FOUR WOMEN AT THE CROSS

Beside the mother of Jesus, there were apparently three other women
standing at the cross; one was her sister, not mentioned by name. The
second was Miriam, the wife of Cleophas, who was the mother of at
least one apostle, James the Less. The third was Miriam of Magdala
(Mary Magdalene), the woman whom Jesus had healed and who loved
Him with a great and sacred love (Lk. 8:2). This Miriam of Magdala
was also privileged to be the first to whom the risen Christ appeared
(Jn. 20:1–2; 11–19).

Four loving hearts, four suffering hearts united in grief under one cross. But the greatest sorrow was that of His mother. Here, truly, the final and most cruel thrust of the sword pierced her soul, even as Simeon had prophesied in the Temple, when, some 33 years before, she held in her arms the child of matchless promise.

In Mark 15:40, Salome is mentioned as one of the women at the cross, in place of "the sister of Miriam" of John 19:25. Again in Matthew 27:56, the mother of the sons of Zebedee is mentioned. If we put the three statements of the three Gospels together, we may reasonably conclude that Salome was the sister of Miriam, the mother of Jesus. Salome was the mother of Zebedee's children; James (to be distinguished from James the Less) and John, the evangelist, who therefore were cousins of Jesus.

This fact should perhaps help explain to us several things. First of all, the reticence of the apostle John to mention the name of the sister of Miriam, simply because she was his mother. We are acquainted with the reticence and the delicacy of John, who refused to mention his own name in the Gospel which he wrote, but referred to himself as "the other disciple whom Jesus loved" (Jn. 20:2; 21:7). For the same reason he did not mention the name of his own mother, but referred to her as "the sister of the mother of Jesus" (19:25). The fact of John's kinship to Jesus may also have some bearing on the question as to why Jesus committed His mother to John.

"WOMAN, BEHOLD THY SON"

When Jesus therefore saw his mother, and the disciple standing by, whom he loved, he saith unto his mother, Woman behold thy son! Then saith he to the disciple, Behold thy mother! And from that hour that disciple took her unto his own home (19:26–27).

Why did Jesus commit His mother to John and not to any of His younger brothers or sisters? One obvious reason would be the fact that, apparently, they were not as yet believers in Him. Their definite conversion seems to have occurred after the resurrection, when the risen Christ appeared also to James, His brother (1 Cor. 15:7). Little is known to us concerning the family circumstances or the material conditions in which these kinsmen of our Lord lived, except as Eusebius tells us, that they were very poor.[2] It is significant that they did not stand with their mother at the cross to comfort her and to uphold her. However, the "beloved disciple," John, was there.

Concerning John we know this: He was a devout disciple of the Lord who loved him in a special way. In all probability, John was a nephew of Miriam, and therefore a cousin of Jesus. He also seems to have been, comparatively, a man of means. We read about John, that he was a partner in some kind of a fishing concern (Lk. 5:7–10). John's father, Zebedee, must have been a man of considerable standing in the community. This may be gathered from the fact that John, "the other disciple," was acquainted with the high priest (Jn. 18:16). The fact that his mother came to Jesus, asking that her sons be made to sit on the right and left side when Jesus would establish His future Kingdom (Mt. 20:20–21) may indicate that the Zebedee family was of some account in Galilee.

Now when the hour had arrived that Jesus should depart from this world there was at the cross (in addition to the women) only John, His beloved disciple. All the others—the apostles and the brethren—fled. Many apparently thought it wiser not to come too close to the cross in order to avoid possible incrimination. The physical brothers and sisters of Jesus, His nearest kinsmen, were also conspicuous by their absence.

It was therefore natural for Jesus to perform His last filial act of devotion by committing His mother to a beloved disciple, who was able and willing to take good care of her. Miriam needed John to help to fill the aching void in her sorrowing heart. The beloved disciple needed Miriam to console him in his unspeakable loss. They needed each other. These two could only show their love and devotion to Him by loving and helping each other, a pattern which Jesus set for His disciples for all times, "That ye love one another; as I have loved you, that ye also love one another" (Jn. 13:34).

This accomplished, all earthly ties of Jesus came to a close. Henceforth Jesus would appear to His disciples regardless of their blood relationship to Him, not as a son, nor as a brother or kinsman, but as their risen Savior and Lord.

The apostle Paul touched upon a deep truth when he wrote: "Wherefore henceforth know we no man after the flesh, yea, though we have known Christ after the flesh, yet now henceforth know we him no more" (2 Cor. 5:16).

CHAPTER SIXTEEN

Miriam in the Upper Room

Then returned they unto Jerusalem from the mount called Olivet, which is from Jerusalem a sabbath day's journey. And when they were come in, they went up into an upper room, where abode Peter, and James, and John, and Andrew, Philip and Thomas, Bartholomew, and Matthew, James the son of Alpheus, and Simon Zelotes, and Judas the brother of James. These all continued with one accord in prayer and supplication with the women, and Mary the mother of Jesus, and with his brethren (Acts 1:12–14).

It is here in the upper room in Jerusalem that we are permitted a last glimpse of Miriam in the pages of the New Testament. It is now after the ascension of Jesus. Actually this is the first time we see her and His brothers in the company of His disciples and followers. Their trysting place was apparently the same upper room mentioned in John 20:19, where the disciples were gathered after the crucifixion, "for fear of the Jews."

But now a radical change has taken place in the hearts and minds of the little flock which followed Jesus. For us contemporaries it is hard to realize the profound impact the resurrection of Christ had upon His disciples and His kinsmen. It at once electrified the disciples, who only a little while before trembled, fearing their own shadow, into a dedicated, ready-for-anything, love-knit fellowship.

The events after the crucifixion had a converting and regenerating effect also upon His brothers who, previous to the resurrection, shied away from Jesus and from His disciples. For the first time they identified themselves with the about-to-be-born *ecclesia*—the fellowship of those who belonged to the body of Christ.

The resurrection of Jesus at last brought healing and comfort to the torn and sorrowing heart of Miriam. Suddenly all the unbearable strains of her life, from the annunciation to the crucifixion, were gone from her being. In spite of all that men did to Him, Jesus was alive, triumphant, and ascended to heaven. From now on nothing else mattered.

Henceforth, Christ would no more be the long-suffering companion of mutually shared travails, not the miracle-working healer of Galilee, nor the wandering, homeless Master-Teacher, who was finally done to death so cruelly. From now on Jesus would be their exalted Lord, who sits on the right hand of God and who is to come again to establish His glorious Kingdom. No fear from within, nor any force from without would now be able to deflect them from proclaiming the Good News about their risen Messiah. If need be, they would gladly lay down their lives for Him. All these people in the upper room were drawn by the mysterious and inexorable power of their risen Lord and by a compelling need for mutual fellowship in prayer and love. Since Jesus had promised that they would "receive power after that the Holy Ghost is come upon you," to enable them to be His witnesses (Acts 1:8), they now prayed for the Holy Spirit to fill them and to prepare them for the task which lay ahead.

They also remembered their Master's promise to return, and the angels' annunciation that "this same Jesus, which is taken up from you into heaven, shall so come in like manner as ye have seen him go into heaven" (v. 11). So they, no doubt, prayed for the speedy return of their beloved Lord and risen Savior.

To these people assembled in the upper room, the imminent return of Christ was a keenly felt personal matter, a consuming longing of their souls. Among these waiting and expectant disciples were also Miriam and the brothers of Jesus.

THE BROTHERS OF JESUS AFTER THE RESURRECTION

The physical kinship to Jesus made it more difficult for His brothers to see in Him the exalted figure of the Messiah, the very personification of Israel's immortal hope. Their physical proximity to their brother Jesus deprived them of the necessary perspective which they needed in order to see Him in all dimensions. It was almost impossible for them to evaluate rightly all that transpired in their midst.

What Jesus foretold concerning others applied with equal force to His physical brothers: "And I, if I be lifted up from the earth, will draw all men unto me" (Jn. 12:32).

While He was yet in their midst there were times when He appeared to them as one who was making exaggerated claims for Himself. At times they even thought that their brother Jesus was "beside Himself." The fact of His resurrection and His appearance to the disciples, and on one occasion to a crowd of 500 people, and again to one of His own brothers (1 Cor. 15:7), revolutionized their whole attitude to Jesus. It transformed their opposition or thinly disguised hostility, into a relationship of complete faith in Him that Jesus was truly the Son of God and their Savior.

For many years the relationship between "the brethren" and Jesus was not unlike the relationship between Joseph and his brethren. They, too, were plagued by a spirit of jealousy, and could not comprehend that God should raise up their own brother Joseph to such an exalted position as to become master over their destinies. Every fiber of their being seemed to revolt against such an idea.

A somewhat similar situation existed between the sons of Jesse and their brother David (1 Sam. 17:28–29). The bitter rivalry, or even the enmity of siblings is a matter of record in history, in psychology, and in common experience among men.

It was the resurrection of Jesus which at last brought His brothers to believe in Him. From now on He would be more than their own flesh and blood. He was their Lord and Savior. The lack of harmony among her own children, which must have often troubled the heart of Miriam, had now vanished. Now they were all of one accord. All tensions and rivalries were forgotten in the mighty surge of faith and the reality of His resurrection.

Except for an indirect reference in Galatians 4:4, this is the last glimpse we have of Miriam. We leave her in a posture of fervent prayer, in the company of her own children, and of His disciples. From here on she passes out of historical sight. Miriam of the New Testament has finished her course gloriously.

From now on, human ingenuity and imagination would gradually seek to transform the Miriam of the New Testament into the Mary of fiction and dogma, a semi-human, semi-divine being, more akin to the female deities of pagan mythology than to the real flesh and blood personality of the Gospels.

Miriam had accomplished her God-appointed task of bringing forth the Messiah of Israel, of nursing and rearing Him through infancy and boyhood. Hers was the privilege of watching, often from afar, over His maturing manhood, as much as Jesus' awareness of His divine origin and task would permit her. In agony of soul Miriam stood at the cross while her beloved son was dying. And now at last she became a devout follower and disciple of Jesus, sharing the faith in Him as risen Lord with countless others of her own and succeeding generations.

Her task completed, Miriam must leave the stage of history unobtrusively, so that her divine son, Jesus, may henceforth shine forth as the Light of the world. From all we have seen of her faith and humility, Miriam would not have wanted this to be otherwise. To ascribe to her honors and powers peculiar only to Jesus, the Son of God, to worship her or to exalt her almost as if she were a divine being, is not to honor her, but to pierce her soul again with a sword. Miriam would have been the first to say, "not unto me, but unto Him be the glory."

"WHERE MARY FELL ASLEEP"

Where today the Church of Dormition is located on Mt. Zion, there, according to Catholic tradition, "Mary fell asleep," and was assumed bodily into heaven. This passing of Mary is referred to as *Koimesis* in Greek or *Transitus Mariae* in Latin, terms used in the early church for the death of the mother of Jesus.[1] This legend became the basis of the dogma of the assumption of Mary.

Thus, a beautiful life came to a glorious finale. It was a life lived in humble faith, in prayer, and in dedicated service to her beloved son and His disciples. For this life every Christian should praise God. In it we have an example of pure, holy, and devout motherhood, a life which found grace and favor in the eyes of God.

Miriam, the lovely Jewish maiden of Nazareth, the virgin mother of our Lord, was the finest and most fragrant flower of Jewish womanhood which had ever blossomed forth from the heart of Jewry. Her prophetic words deserved to become true: "Henceforth all generations shall call me blessed" (Lk. 1:48).

Long after Miriam's death, gradually out of her blessed memory a new and alien image emerged, molded and fashioned by the still-potent forces of ancient myths and cults dedicated to the worship of the Great Mother, the goddess of life and fertility. To the Egyptians she was known as Isis, to the Babylonians as Ishtar, to the Greeks as Cybele, or Demeter, or Diana. The Romans worshiped her as Minerva. All these cults had deep and intertwining roots among the pagan peoples around the shores of the Mediterranean. Between the Miriam of New Testament history and the Mary of myth, legend, and Marian dogma, there is a gap which no human ingenuity or pious invention will ever be able to bridge.

PART THREE

Miriam in Post-Biblical Traditions

CHAPTER SEVENTEEN

Transformation of Miriam Into Mary

"Sirs, Why Do Ye These Things?"

The Bible-oriented Christian must marvel at the way in which the mother of our Lord has, in Roman Catholic piety and dogma, gradually been lifted out of her humanity and elevated to the position of a quasi deity. In spite of repeated denials, Mary has, to a considerable extent, replaced Christ Himself in the affection and devotion of millions of people. Like the apostle Paul at Lystra, the baffled and disconcerted Christian is inclined to cry out, "Sirs, why do ye these things?"

The growing cult of Mary has caused a deep and ever-widening rift in Christendom. There is a considerable element of truth in the remark attributed to the famous British statesman, Benjamin Disraeli: "Half of Christendom worships a Jewish man, and the other half a Jewish woman."

What then were the forces which gradually transformed the humble Jewish virgin of Nazareth, Miriam, into Mary, Mother of God and Queen of Heaven? What were the ideas and the driving instincts in the thinking of so many which caused Mary to become "the dispenser of grace and mediatrix of salvation," and the central figure in the affection and adoration of millions? In the following chapters we shall seek to find an answer to this perplexing question, which perhaps more than any other theological issue has divided Christendom and caused a deep rift within the church.

THE LYSTRA INCIDENT

In Acts 14 we read about a strange experience of the apostle Paul and Barnabas in the city of Lystra in Asia Minor. There, in the course of his itinerant ministry, Paul healed a man who was lame from his birth, and then this is what happened:

> *And when the people saw what Paul had done, they lifted up their voices, saying in the speech of Lycaonia, The gods are come down to us in the likeness of men. And they called Barnabas Jupiter (Zeus); and Paul, Mercurius (Hermes), because he was the chief speaker. Then the priest of Jupiter, which was before their city, brought oxen and garlands unto the gates, and would have done sacrifice with the people. Which when the apostles, Barnabas and Paul, heard of, they rent their clothes, and ran in among the people, crying out, and saying, Sirs, why do ye these things? We also are men of like passions with you, and preach unto you that ye should turn from these vanities unto the living God, which made heaven, and earth, and the sea, and all things that are therein. Who in times past suffered all nations to walk in their own ways.*
>
> *Nevertheless he left not himself without witness, in that he did good, and gave us rain from heaven, and fruitful seasons, filling our hearts with food and gladness. And with these sayings scarce restrained they the people, that they had not done sacrifice unto them* (Acts 14 :11-18).

There could hardly have been anything more disconcerting to Paul and Barnabas, raised in the tradition of strict biblical monotheism, than to be taken for gods. And yet, to the inhabitants of Lystra, nurtured on Greek mythology, nothing came more natural than just that. It took all the eloquence of Paul and Barnabas, with their intense expression of horror, to dissuade these well-meaning but misguided people from sacrificing to them, and from honoring them as gods.

This incident reflects the wide gap which has always existed between Jewish thinking, nurtured in biblical monotheism, and the Greek mind, steeped in a world of gods and semi-divine human beings.

The experience of Paul and Barnabas explains in some measure what happened to Miriam after her death. To the newly Christianized people of the Hellenic and Roman world, it was natural and almost inevitable that they should, with the passing of time, begin to transform the humble Jewish maiden, Miriam, the mother of Christ, into a semi-divine being, conforming to the image of their own goddesses which they had worshiped from time immemorial.

GODDESSES

The ancient world of the Semitic, Egyptian, Greek, and Roman civilizations abounded in gods and goddesses, which personified the forces of fertility, of spring and awakening new life. To the Semitic peoples the goddess of fertility was known as Ishtar or Astarte; the Egyptians worshiped her as Isis, the spouse of Osiris; the Greeks worshiped her as Athena, Demeter, Cybele or Diana. To the Romans she was known as Juno or Minerva. To all of them she was familiar as the Great Mother or Queen of Heaven. Even the Israelites, in spite of their strong monotheistic heritage, succumbed to this all-pervading and insidious cult, apparently brought by them from Egypt. This cult was especially popular among the women (Jer. 44:17, 25).

If this cult was able to exert such a potent influence on monotheistic Jews, how much more pervasive must its impact have been upon the newly baptized and only superficially converted pagans?

When Christianity spread throughout the Roman Empire around the shores of the Mediterranean, the forces of paganism were still very strong. Under this influence a gradual and subtle transformation took place, whereby Mary replaced the old goddesses in the devotion of the new converts. At the same time, shrines dedicated to Mary began to replace the ancient temples of her former pagan rivals. The old saying, *Victi victoribus leges diderunt*—"The conquered imposed their laws (or, as in this case their cults) upon the conquerors," was certainly true in this situation.

Although Christianity was superficially victorious, paganism remained deep-rooted and would not surrender without a stubborn and protracted battle. In fact, paganism never fully surrendered to Christianity. Imperceptibly and subtly, it survived and strongly influenced the early church, its institutions, its doctrines and its mode of worship. Although the tree of paganism was cut down, the roots remained deep in the soil and helped transform Miriam of the Gospels into Mary of popular piety—later into mariological dogma.

THE QUEEN OF HEAVEN

In the second century AD, the story of Apuleius called *Metamorphoses* or *The Golden Ass,* indicates quite clearly the interrelationship between the ancient cult of the Mediterranean goddesses and the cult of Mary.

According to that story; Lucius Apuleius, a young Roman nobleman of Madaura in North Africa, in consequence of his romantic indiscretions, became transformed into a donkey by a vengeful witch. This involved Apuleius in various unpleasant adventures. Seeking release from his predicament, Apuleius was directed to the Egyptian goddess Isis, whom he entreated to restore him to his previous human form. In answer to Apuleius' supplication, Isis appeared to him out of the sea and addressed him in this manner:

> Behold me, Lucius, moved by thy prayers. I am the Mother of Nature, Mistress of all the elements, first Progenetrix of the ages, Supreme among the divinities, Queen of the dead, First of the Celestial Beings, Figure alike of Gods and Goddesses. With my nod I govern the heights of heaven in their brightness, the health-bringing winds of the sea, the mournful silences of the underworld. My divinity in its uniqueness is worshiped by all the world in many forms, by various rites, under diverse names. The Phrygians, first-born among the peoples, call me Mother of the Gods of Pessinus, the autochthonous Athenians, Minerva Cecrops; the islanders of Cyprus, Venus Paphia, the Cretans who draw the bow Dianna Ductynna; the Sicilians who speak three tongues, Stygian Proserpina, the Eleusinians, the ancient Goddess Ceres; some call me Juno, others Bellona, Hecate, Ramnusia. The Ethiopians, lighted by the first rays of the rising sun, and the Arii, and the Egyptians wise through ancient lore, honor me with rites that are proper to me, and call me by my true name, Isis Regina!

Having obtained an answer to his prayer, Apuleius thus expressed his gratitude:

> O thou Holy one, perpetual savior of mankind, always bountiful in nourishing mortals, thou dost give a mother's sweet affection to the wretched and unfortunate. No day goes by, no night, no

slightest moment that is empty of thy benefits or that thy protection is not over men by sea and land. Thou dost assuage the tempests of our life. Thou dost hold out thy helping hand and drawest out the tangled threads of the Fates; thou calmest the storms of Fortune and restrainest the stars in their hurtful course. The supernal beings honor thee, the infernal deities do thee reverence; thou dost make the world revolve and to the Sun thou givest its light; thou dost rule the world and hast the powers of hell under thy feet. The stars obey thee, by thee the seasons come again, in thee the gods are joyful and the elements are thy servants. At thy nod the winds blow gently and clouds gather, seed comes to life and crops grow up. The birds of heaven fear before thy majesty and the wild bears of the hills, the serpents hiding in the earth and the monsters swimming in the deep. To celebrate thy praises my talent cannot suffice.[1]

Just as in later Marian piety, Isis is here invoked as the savior of mankind, the sweet protector of the wretched and unfortunate, as Queen of heaven and Earth and of the nether regions below.

The historian Plutarch mentions the following inscription in the temple of Sais dedicated to the goddess Isis: "I am all that has been and is and is to be, and no mortal has taken away my virtue" (Plutarch, *De Iside et Ostride,* chap. 2).

As we have already mentioned, the cult of the Queen of Heaven goes back to time immemorial. Even Israel from time to time succumbed to this form of idolatry.

The prophet Jeremiah, in the sixth century BC, thus describes this cult:

The children gather wood, and the fathers kindle the fire, and the women knead their dough, to make cakes to the queen of heaven, and to pour out drink offerings unto other gods, that they may provoke me to anger.

Do they provoke me to anger? saith the LORD: Do they not provoke themselves to the confusion of their own faces? (Jer. 7:18–19).

Apparently the people of Israel sometimes attributed their prosperity to the worship of the Queen of Heaven as the goddess of fertility.

> *But we will certainly do whatsoever thing goeth forth out of our*
> *own mouth, to burn incense unto the queen of heaven, and to pour*
> *out drink offerings unto her, as we have done, we, and our fathers,*
> *our kings and our princes, in the cities of Judah, and in the streets*
> *of Jerusalem; for then had we plenty of victuals, and were well and*
> *saw no evil.*

> *Thus saith the LORD of hosts, the God of Israel, saying: Ye and*
> *your wives have both spoken with your mouths, and fulfilled with*
> *your hand, saying, we will surely perform our vows that we have*
> *vowed, to burn incense to the queen of heaven, and to pour out*
> *drink offerings unto her; ye will surely accomplish your vows, and*
> *surely perform your vows* (Jer. 44:17, 25).

The worship of the Queen of Heaven among the children of Israel constituted a manifest relapse from monotheism into idolatry.

The similarity between the cult of the Queen of Heaven in the days of Jeremiah and the cult of Mary in later times is fairly obvious. The gods and goddesses of antiquity die hard.

GNOSTICISM

Another trend which made its contribution toward the cult of Mary was gnosticism, especially in its Christian form. This religio-philosophical movement sought to attain redemption by a superior and mystical form of knowledge.

Gnosticism which was influenced by Platonic and neo-Platonic ideas, had its own rather weird theology of creation in which Adam and Eve played a cosmic role.

According to gnostic cosmogony, Adam, the First Man, identified with the Universal Father, begot the Son of Man, or the Second Man, or Christ, also called the Logos. The Spirit (Hebrew, *Ruach*), which brooded over the face of the earth was the First Woman. She became the Mother of Christ. Out of the First Woman emanated Sophia—*Khokhma*—Wisdom, which created the wicked world of senses and matter. One of the seven powers emanating from Sophia was Ialdabaoth who seduced Eve. When later Eve repented, the First Woman had compassion on her, and prayed to the First Man to send the Son Christ to help her.

Christ came down, and together with Sophia made their dwelling in the most pure and holy man Jesus, born of the Virgin Mary. They remained in Him until He was crucified. According to gnostic teaching, only the *man* Jesus was crucified and was then raised up by the son Christ (Irenaeus Adversus Haereses, book I, chap. 30).

In this weird speculation, Mary the virgin mother of Jesus became associated with the eternal Mother of Christ, identified with Sophia—Wisdom, thus forming one super-human being.

Officially the Church rejected these gnostic speculations. However, the heretical movements of the third and fourth centuries carried the identification of Mary the Virgin Mother of Jesus and the celestial Mother of Christ to its completion.

"The Church Father Epiphanius, at the end of the fourth century, in his catalogue of heresies mentions a sect of women in Arabia, of Thracian origin, who offered to the Virgin little cakes of barley flour and called themselves by the title 'priestesses of Mary.'"[2]

It is significant that at the end of the fourth century Epiphanius rejected the cult of Mary with indignation, declaring that she is not a goddess and sacrifices were not to be made to her. Only after the Council of Ephesus in 431 was the ground prepared for the worship of Mary, not just in peripheral, sectarian Christianity, but in the mainstream of Christendom, in the Catholic Church.

THEOTOKOS-MOTHER OF GOD

An important stage in the Marian cult was reached with the official adoption by the Council of Nicea of the Greek term *theotokos*—Mother of God, as a description of Mary. This term gained wide currency during the heated disputes of the third and fourth centuries concerning the two natures of Christ—the human and the divine. The Council of Nicea in 325, after condemning the anti-trinitarian position of Arius, affirmed the perfect divinity of Christ. God the Son, the Council declared, was "consubstantial" with the Father. Henceforth Mary was to be considered as *theotokos*—the Mother of God. The purpose of this title was not to glorify Mary, but rather to express the belief that the eternal God humbled Himself and came down into the world "in the form of a servant" (Phil. 2:7), and was born of the virgin Mary. However, the term *theotokos* was pregnant with possibilities of misinterpretation and mischief, which later history proved only too abundantly.

The exact meaning and significance of *theotokos* was disputed with vehemence and venom at the Councils of Ephesus in 431 and Chalcedon in 451.

The point of dispute was not Mary, but Christ. How was one to understand that God was crucified or that God was born of the virgin Mary?

Nestorius, bishop of Constantinople, found the term *theotokos* misleading because God cannot be born, nor can He die, but Christ the Son of God was born and did die on the cross. He therefore proposed that Mary should be called *Christotokos*—the Mother of Christ. His opponent, Cyril, bishop of Alexandria, who championed the complete and perfect union of the human and divine nature of Christ insisted on the term *theotokos*, that Mary was the Mother of God.

To speak of Mary as the "Mother of God," Nestorius maintained, makes the Christian doctrine ridiculous in the eyes of pagans, because God cannot be born.

In spite of the objections of Nestorius, the Council of Ephesus confirmed the title *theotokos* as orthodox and proper.

What to the theologians assembled at Ephesus was a theological formula designed to express the perfect union of the human and divine natures of Christ, to the common people, especially to the inhabitants of Ephesus, became a question of local pride, honor, and piety. It must be remembered that according to local tradition, Mary died in Ephesus and her tomb was shown as being located not far from the tomb of the apostle John. It is hard to say how much this strong local sentiment for Mary influenced the outcome of the Council of Ephesus in 431. It should also be remembered that Ephesus was the city where the apostle Paul was nearly lynched by an incensed mob of worshipers of the Great Goddess Diana (Acts 19:23–24).

After confirming the position of the Council of Nicea, the Council of Ephesus declared: "We confess that the Holy Virgin is Mother of God (*theotokos*), by the fact that God the Word is incarnated and made man, and from her conception has united to his very self the temple taken from her."[3]

It was this formula *theotokos* which became the doctrinal foundation for the cult of Mary. Thus it can be said that in the year 431 official sanction was given to the Marian cult, which at first was only a popular expression of a Mary-centered piety, but later became the basis of church dogma.

THE ABSORPTION OF PAGAN ELEMENTS

The Council of Ephesus gave renewed impetus to the absorption of pagan elements into the cult of Mary. From then on Mary was depicted in various forms of art as the enthroned virgin who holds her son just as Isis holds her son Horus on her knees. Like the Greek goddess Cybele, Mary was henceforth portrayed as wearing the crown of Magna Mater.

At about this time we meet with the practice of erecting churches dedicated to Mary, built on the foundation of ancient pagan deities. For instance, the church of Santa Maria Antique in Rome was built on the ruins of the temple dedicated to Pallas Athena, and Santa Maria Maggiore was built on the site of the temple of Cybele—the Mother of Gods.

This building of churches dedicated to Mary followed a spontaneous substitution by the masses of recently "converted" pagans of a new devotion dedicated to Mary for the devotion to their former goddesses. The Mariologist Cocchelli in his *Mater Christi*, page 150 writes:

> *The contribution of the pagan devotion to the female divinities was a factor that was subsequently to make itself felt more strongly in manifestations of popular piety....On the other hand it cannot be denied that in the impulse it took at a particular moment, the cult of the Madonna may have been part of that general turning of Mediterranean deference toward the heavenly woman, Virgin or Mother or else an associate in a love toward the heavenly woman, Virgin or Mother or else an associate in a love mystery.*[4]

CHAPTER EIGHTEEN

The Immaculate Conception

There are two distinct elements which have been decisive in forming the cult of Mary:

1. At first there was a popular devotion to Mary and a piety which centered around her person.
2. Then, some 15 centuries later, came the official and formal dogmas of the Church defining the position of Mary in doctrine.

Thus far there are two such dogmas pertaining to Mary:

1. The Immaculate Conception of the Virgin Mary.
2. The bodily Assumption of Mary into heaven.

On December 8, 1854, Pope Pius IX in the bull *Ineffabilis Deus* defined the Immaculate Conception in this manner.

> *In honor of the Holy and Indivisible Trinity, for the decor and ornament of the Virgin Mother of God, for the exultation of the Catholic faith and the Christian religion, by the authority of our Lord Jesus Christ and of the blessed Apostles Peter and Paul, and by Ours, we declare, pronounce and define the doctrine according to which the Most Blessed Virgin Mary in the first instant of her conception by the singular grace and privilege of the Almighty, and in consideration of the merits of Christ Jesus the Savior of the human race, was preserved immune from all stain of original sin, is revealed by God and therefore is to be believed firmly and constantly by all faithful.*

The dogma of the Immaculate Conception of Mary is the culmination of more than 15 centuries of pious opinions, of fervent Marian devotion and of controversies, which centered around the question whether Mary, in common with the rest of humanity was affected by the consequence of original sin.

Already, Origen of Alexandria (185-254) attributed to Mary a special measure of sanctity. Nevertheless, Origen held that Mary was not perfect, that she too was numbered among those of whom Christ predicted that they would be offended at Him. Like the apostles, she too was discouraged and confused by the cross. She therefore sinned, but was redeemed by the death of Christ.[1]

John Chrysostom, the famous Greek Father (345-407) was of the opinion that at the wedding of Cana, Mary was not immune from maternal vanity.

In the fourth century, Ambrose of Milan idealized Mary as the perfect picture of virginity. However, none of the Church fathers saw in Mary anything more than a much-favored person and saint. The idea of her sinlessness became an issue later in the fifth century.

In the controversy concerning the doctrine of original sin between Pelagius (360-420) and Augustine (354-430) in the fifth century, Pelagius maintained that already in the Old Testament some saints of God were without sin. Why, then, he reasoned, should not this apply to the Virgin Mary? On the other hand, Augustine was of the opinion that none of the Old Testament saints was free from sin, but "I make an exception for the Virgin Mary, about whom for the honor due to the Lord, I do not want to have any discussion when it concerns sin, since we know that she who has been worthy to conceive and bear Him who was without sin, has received a greater grace to conquer sin completely."[2] It is significant that Augustine was of the opinion that Mary was born without sin and not that she was conceived without sin.

Elsewhere he maintained that Mary received her physical body through the tainted line of Adam "through the sin of propagation," in an apparent allusion to Psalm 51:5, "Behold I was shapen in iniquity, and in sin did my mother conceive me."

This condition, however, was according to Augustine, remedied by a greater measure of grace which enabled her to overcome sin.

Opinion among Catholic theologians concerning Mary's exemption from the condemnation of original sin varied considerably. Some (like Paschasius Radbertus) declared that she was uncorrupted and uncontaminated and free from all contagion of conception as a result of her sanctification in her mother's womb. This was assumed on the basis of a parallel with the prophet Jeremiah, who was consecrated from his mother's womb (Jer. 1:5). A similar analogy was seen in the person of John the Baptist, who was filled with the Holy Ghost from his mother's womb (Lk. 1:15).

On the other hand, Anselm of Canterbury (1033-1109) taught that Mary was conceived and born in sin just like all other children of Adam.

When in 1140 the Feast of the Immaculate Conception of Mary was introduced in the city of Lyons, Bernard of Clairvaux wrote a stinging letter rebuking those responsible for the unseemly innovation. His opposition was not prompted by any lack of devotion to Mary, but rather by his disdain for a false, unscriptural piety, which not adding to Mary, diminished Christ. Here are a few passages from his letter:

> *The royal Virgin has no need of a false honor, being well supplied with authentic titles of glory....I say that she gloriously conceived by the Holy Spirit, but was not conceived of it; I say that she has given birth as a Virgin, but was not born by a Virgin. If not, where is the prerogative of the Mother of the Lord...?"*

> *This was not to honor the Virgin, but to diminish her honor....*

> *Only Jesus Christ then was conceived by the Holy Spirit, since He alone was sanctified before and after conception. Except for Him, the sons of Adam are in the position that one of them truly and humbly confessed himself, 'I was conceived in iniquity and in sin did my mother conceive me'.*[3]

Thomas Aquinas (the Angelic Doctor), in his famous *Summa Theologica* declared that he believed that the Virgin was sanctified in her mother's womb, but that was not a truth revealed in the Bible. He maintained that the Immaculate Conception can be shown rationally as implied in the angelic greeting *Ave Maria gratia plena,* from the example of Jeremiah 1:5; of John the Baptist, Luke 1:15. This, however, was not in his opinion a revealed truth but a theological proposition.

Thomas taught that the incitement to concupiscence, the root of all sins, and the main consequence of original sin, was in the case of Mary bound or held in check by the abundance of grace. But she was not freed from death nor from other penal sanctions of original sin.

Similarly, Bonaventura (Giovanni di Fidanza, 1221-1274) maintained that Mary contracted original sin and consequently suffered the penalty and sorrow of death. However, she was sanctified before giving birth.

Thus the three great theologians of the 12th and 13th centuries, Anselm, Bernard, and Thomas Aquinas, while accepting Mary's sanctification in her mother's womb, rejected the idea of Immaculate Conception.

The first opinion concerning Mary's sanctification purported to see an analogy with presumed biblical precedence (Jeremiah, John the Baptist), whereas the doctrine of the Immaculate Conception breaks the precedence and elevates Mary into a unique position of honor.

The teaching of the Immaculate Conception came too close for comfort to the New Testament teaching concerning the miraculous, supernatural conception of Jesus. This is what made the great theologians so uneasy.

It must be pointed out that the supposed analogy between Mary and Jeremiah or John the Baptist cannot be upheld in the light of any reasonable interpretation of the respective scriptural passages. Concerning Jeremiah we read: "Then the word of the LORD came unto me, saying, before I formed thee in the belly I knew thee; and before thou camest forth out of the womb I sanctified thee, and I ordained thee a prophet unto the nations" (Jer. 1:4–5).

Here the reference is to Jeremiah's consecration for a particular mission, without any reference to being set free from sin, whether original or actual.

Neither can the analogy of John the Baptist be taken seriously.

"And he will be filled with the Holy Spirit even from his mother's womb" (Lk. 1:15). Here John the Baptist was promised the Holy Spirit for the purpose of his prophetic mission, but no immunity from original sin was granted to him.

Behind the doctrine of the Immaculate Conception was the medieval idea that sexual ascetism and virginal purity was the highest expression of perfection. It was the ideal of medieval monasteries and nunneries, but not the perfection of biblical womanhood. As we have already seen, the ideal biblical woman was the perfect wife and mother of children.

By the 17th century the belief in the Immaculate Conception became so entrenched and popular that Pope Alexander VII declared that it is an ancient and pious judgment that "Mary's soul in the first instant of its creation and infusion into the body, by special grace and privilege of God, and in consideration of the merits of Christ, was preserved immune from all stains and original sin."

In 1708 the Feast of the Immaculate Conception was extended to the whole Church.

In the papal definition of the Immaculate Conception, this dogma was called "revealed truth." The Catholic Church teaches that a truth can be contained in the Scripture either explicitly (directly) or implicity (indirectly).

The dogma of the Immaculate Conception is based on such an implicit "truth." In consequence of this position, "truth" is anything the Church teaches as being true. Calvin, discussing the teaching concerning the Immaculate Conception acidly remarked: "There is no fiction so silly that it may not be considered an article of faith by jack-asses."[4]

The dogma of the Immaculate Conception, like the pronouncement of the Council of Ephesus in 431 about the *theotokos,* was of utmost importance to the Marian cult.

From then on she was considered through the grace received from birth as being superior to all the saints and angels put together.

By virtue of the Immaculate Conception she had all the gifts of the Holy Spirit in fullness; she possessed all the knowledge and all the perfections of body, mind, and spirit.

All the sluices for her glorification were from now on opened.

CHAPTER NINETEEN

The Assumption of Mary

On August 15, 1950, Pope Pius XII promulgated the dogma of the Assumption of Virgin Mary.

This dogma makes it an article of the Catholic faith that Mary by virtue of being free from the consequences of original sin, did not succumb to death like other sons of Adam, but that her body was taken up alive unto heaven, where she sits on the right hand of Christ.

The papal bull, *Munificentissimus Deus,* in which the dogma was promulgated, endeavors to substantiate this doctrine with biblical proof, which we will discuss later.

But the main basis of the dogma is the Authority of the Church.

The Church, the bull declares, has the mandate to preserve and to transmit the truth pure and unchanged. Therefore, from the universal consensus of the Church can be drawn a sure and certain argument for affirming the Assumption. "It is a truth revealed of God."

Again the authority of the Church is invoked as proof of the truth—a hopeless vicious circle. "It is true because Rome says so, Rome says so because it is true."

THE TRADITIONS BEHIND THE ASSUMPTION

The dogma of the Assumption has been some 18 centuries in the making. It started with legends and myths apparently related to Indian, Babylonian, Greek, and other Mediterranean myths and mysteries. These in turn became the core of popular Marian piety and worship. Finally, under the incessant pressure of such piety, at the grass roots, upon the highest ecclesiastical authorities, the pious belief of the masses was pronounced a dogma.

In the previous chapter we have mentioned a sect in Arabia which

worshiped Mary, and was known as the Collyrydians. At the end of
the fourth century, Epiphanius, writing against this cult, admonished
them in the following manner:

*Search the Scriptures, you will not find either the death of Mary
or whether she did or did not die, or that she was buried or not
buried. The body of Mary is holy, but she is not God. She is virgin
and worthy of great honor, but she is not given to us in adoration,
rather she adores Him, who was born of her flesh.*[1]

Apparently by that time the tradition concerning Mary's departure
from this life was not yet fixed.

However, by the middle of the fifth century, the tradition that Mary
died in Jerusalem and that her sepulcher was in Gethsemane became
established.

There was great curiosity among Christians concerning the life and
death of Mary. Since there was no authentic information, imagination
ran wild creating legends.

In the fifth century a document called *Transitus Mariae* began to
circulate. This legendary story of the Passing of Mary was based on an
older second century apocryphal document *Koimesis*, or the Falling
Asleep of the Holy Mother of God. The *Transitus* is also known as
the *Pseudo-Melito*.

There was also another version of the *Transitus* attributed to the
apostle John.

Pope Pelagius (492-496) condemned the *Transitus* together with
other apocryphal stories of this character.

According to both versions of the *Transitus Mariae*, which differ in
numerous details, the essence of the legend is this:

An angel announced to Mary that she would die on Friday in her
home in Bethlehem. She prayed at the sepulcher of Jesus and asked
that the apostles should come and help her. They did. John came on
a cloud from Ephesus. Andrew, Philip, Luke, and Simon rose from
their graves and the rest of the apostles were transported on a cloud to
Bethlehem. Jesus appeared accompanied by a heavenly host. He told
Mary that her body would be taken to Paradise on Earth and her soul
would be received into heaven.

Mary asked Jesus to grant her a last request, that every soul which shall ever pray invoking her intercession, shall find mercy and consolation in this life and in the next. Jesus granted her this request.

Mary blessed the apostles and placed her soul in the hands of Jesus. During her funeral rites which followed her *transitus,* Gophonias a Jew wanted to overturn her bier, but his hands were cut off by an angel. Gophonias prayed in Mary's name and he was healed again.

Mary was laid in a new sepulcher at Gethsemane. She remained there three days, then her body was carried into Paradise to join Elisabeth, Anna, Abraham, Isaac, and Jacob. *Pseudo-Melito* and *Pseudo-John* differ in numerous details.

In later centuries there were a number of apocryphal stories of a similar character. All of them agree that Mary's soul was taken to heaven but differ about her body, whether it remained uncorrupted or whether it was "assumed" to heaven. It is significant that these legends either deliberately or unconsciously seek to make the passing of Mary similar to the death of Christ.

John of Damascus (died 749) was of the opinion that the doctrine of the Assumption has no basis in Scripture or in history, but that her body was preserved in a state of incorruption, because it was "becoming" (Greek, *edei;* Latin, *decuit*) that the Mother of God should be so honored by her Son.

The argument of "becoming"—of being suitable or proper—is of great importance in later Catholic theology, and has been often used as "proof" for the justification of certain dogmas. The reasoning was along the lines of this questionable syllogism:

Potuit, decuit, fecit. God can do all things.

It is proper that it should be so; Therefore God did it.

The fallacy of this syllogism is obvious. It assumes that men can decide what is "suitable" or "proper" in God's eyes. It sets up human reasoning as a basis for arriving at dogmatic truth, without a scriptural foundation, or even against the express testimony of the Bible.

Of great importance for the dogma of the Assumption were also two other spurious documents of the ninth century, the Epistle of Pseudo-Jerome and the Book of Pseudo-Augustine.

In the Epistle of Pseudo-Jerome the conviction is expressed that Mary died and that her sepulcher is in the Valley of Jehoshophat in

Jerusalem; that she was buried there, but now her sepulcher is empty. Because of this, some people wonder whether she was assumed alive with her body into heaven or whether she left her body behind. Pseudo-Jerome concludes: "It is better to leave all these things to God to Whom nothing is impossible, rather than to seek with temerity to define on our authority things we cannot prove."[2]

The Pseudo-Augustine document takes this position:

> *Christ the power of God and the wisdom of God...wills all things that are just and right. In consequence it seems right that Mary enjoys unutterable happiness in body and soul in her Son, with her Son, through her Son—and that she must not have suffered corruption, she who did not become subject to any corruption in giving birth to such a Son.*

> *It seems right that she should always continue incorrupt.... I do not dare to speak otherwise, not daring to think otherwise.*[3]

The above opinions of the two spurious documents dominated Catholic thinking in the matter of the Assumption during the Middle Ages right into modern times. It was not the work of great theologians which finally led to the promulgation of the Assumption, but rather the pressure of the pious masses, which increased steadily with the passing of time.

Between 1920 and 1940 this pressure assumed the character of a regular campaign for the Assumption. More than 8 million votes were collected, mostly in Spain, Italy, and Latin America, petitioning the Pope to define the dogma of the Assumption.

So much for the traditions upon which this dogma is based.

Now for the "biblical proofs."

The most important of these proofs are three:

"I will put enmities between thee and the woman, and between thy seed and her seed; she shall crush thy head, and thou shalt lie in wait for her heel" (Gen. 3:15, Douay Version).

This prophecy is interpreted as the victory of Christ over sin, the wages of which is death. And since Mary is inseparable from Christ, therefore this is a promise of Mary's victory over death.

"And the angel came in unto her, and said, Hail thou that art highly favored, the Lord is with thee; blessed art thou among women"(Lk. 1:28). If Mary is full of grace, she cannot, according to Catholic reasoning be subject to death.

"And there appeared a great wonder in heaven; a woman clothed with the sun, and the moon under her feet, and upon her head a crown of twelve stars" (Rev. 12:1). The woman clothed with the sun is Mary, according to Catholic theologians.

The dogma of the Assumption ignores the statement in Revelation 12:14 that the woman escaped before the serpent into the wilderness, which does not fit the description of Mary.

Protestant theologians have considered the woman clothed with the sun either as a type of Israel or as representing the Church.

The bull *Munificentissimus Deus,* realizing the feebleness both of Catholic tradition concerning the Assumption and of the "biblical proof," seeks to fortify the dogma with the authority of the Church. A vicious circle! Spurious traditions and spurious biblical proofs are supposed to prove the authority of the Church, and in turn, this authority is supposed to confirm the traditions and the "proofs."

In the final analysis, the dogma implies that revealed truth is what the Church declares.

THE ARGUMENT OF "SUITABILITY"

A final element in support of the dogma is the argument of "suitability."

Mary, according to this reasoning, is the Mother of God; as such she was immaculately conceived and was a virgin perpetually. She is also associated with Christ in the work of redemption as coredemptress (although this dogma still remains to be promulgated). Therefore it is *suitable* that she should be associated with Him in the resurrection.

It is also considered that the dogma of the Assumption helps the faithful in their devotion to Mary and to Christ.

Explaining over the Rome radio the significance of the Assumption, the Catholic theologian G. M. Roschini quoted 1 Corinthians 15:21–22, adding to it:

"Since by man and woman (Adam and Eve) came death, so by man and woman (Christ and Mary) came life, the resurrection of the dead."

Such are the "proofs" that Mary was raised with Christ three days after her death and has been bodily assumed to heaven.

CHAPTER TWENTY

Mary the Co-Redemptress

I n his first letter to Timothy 2:5 the apostle Paul declares:
"For there is one God, and one Mediator between God and men, the man Christ Jesus" (2:5).

This passage seems to be plain in its meaning and does not leave any room for an additional redeemer, whether male or female. Nevertheless, by a long process of mariological speculation and popular piety, new dogmas have been promulgated by the Church of Rome which, carried to their logical conclusion, make the future declaration of Mary as Co-Redemptress inevitable.[1]

The main theme of contemporary Mariology is the role of Mary in the work of redemption. This subject has been vigorously promoted by many Popes of the 19th and 20th centuries, and is currently being investigated by numerous theologians.[2]

Since the Council of Trent (1545-1563), the official position of the Catholic Church has been that in addition to the Scriptures which are the inspired and infallible Word of God, the traditions of the Church are also the foundation of the true faith.

The Church has the sole authority of interpreting the Scriptures and of deciding what is genuine tradition and what should be considered spurious. Protestants often make the mistake of asking for scriptural proof for various Catholic doctrines, without realizing that to the Catholic Church, tradition is also an adequate source and foundation of her teachings. Nevertheless, the Church gives preference to scriptural proof where she can, bolstering her arguments further with her traditions.

What then are the "scriptural proofs" for Co-Redemption?

1. The Seed of the Woman.

"I will put enmities between thee and the woman, and between thy

seed and her seed; she shall crush thy head, and thou shalt lie in wait
for her heel" (Gen. 3:15, Douay Version).

For comparison we quote the same passage from the King James
Version, which is more true to the original Hebrew text:

"And I will put enmity between thee and the woman, and between
thy seed and her seed; it shall bruise thy head, and thou shalt bruise
his heel."

In the bull *Ineffabilis Deus*, which we have already mentioned in
connection with the dogma of the Immaculate Conception, Pope Pius
IX, referring to Genesis 3:15 in the garbled Latin translation of the
Vulgate, declared:

> *She (Mary) was united with Him (Christ) by the closest and
> indissoluble bond and through Him she exercised an everlasting
> enmity against the poisonous serpent, and triumphing over him
> completely bruised his head with her immaculate heel.*[3]

Back in the second century Irenaeus saw in this passage a parallel
between Eve and Mary, a parallel which was to result in far-reaching
consequences in the development of Mariology.

In his famous work *Adversus Haereses*, III, chapter 22, Irenaeus
remarked: "Eve disobedient, became the cause of death for herself and
all the human race. Mary, obedient became the cause of salvation for
herself and the human race."

2. "Be It Unto Me."

Another key passage used in Mariology to support the idea of Mary's
active participation in the work of redemption is the Lukan record of
the Annunciation (1:26–38). The weight of the argument there rests
especially upon verse 38: "And Mary said: Behold the handmaid of the
Lord, be it unto me according to thy word."

We have already discussed this passage in connection with the
Annunciation.[4]

In Catholic thought, Mary's "Be it unto me according to thy word,"
takes on cosmic proportions. Her answer to the angel's annunciation
is not interpreted as an expression of Mary's submission to God's will,
but as a free choice between her acceptance of a mission of extreme
sorrow—or the perdition of mankind. If Mary, they argue, had refused

the annunciation—there would have been no redemption. Her "so be it" made possible the incarnation and the subsequent redemption of mankind.

In Catholic thought, "Mary stands in the midst as Mediatrix of reconciliation between God and men."[5]

The non-Catholic student of Mariology who tries to follow its shaky premises and strained conclusions finds himself in a kind of theological *Alice in Wonderland* in which things, in spite of their seeming logic, become "curiouser and curiouser."

Hermann Volk, a German Mariologist in his study *Christus und Maria* states: "The Holy Scriptures themselves link Mary and Christ together in the words which became a part of the Ave Maria: 'Blessed art thou and blessed is the fruit of thy womb'"(Lk. 1:42).[6]

Characteristically Volk devotes a whole chapter to explain the little word *and*, which links the phrase *Christ and Mary.*

But the link *and* is structurally too weak to bear the full weight of meaning which Mariology puts upon it.

Catholic theology seems agreed that Mary had a share in the redemption of humanity. The only question it seeks to answer is, What was the nature of this participation in the work of redemption? Was the participation of an indirect, passive and subjective nature, that is *de congruo,* or was her mediation of a direct, immediate, objective character similar to that of Christ Himself, referred to in Catholic theology as *de condigno?*

At present most Mariologists are of the opinion that Mary, by her compassion and by joining her own sufferings to the suffering of Jesus, has subjectively participated in our salvation. Nevertheless more and more Mariologists tend towards the position that Mary's participation in the work of redemption was immediate and direct; that she is in association with Christ as the Co-Redemptress of men in the primary sense of the word.

3. Stabat Mater.

A third key passage used in support of Mary's mediatorship is John 19:25–27. This is how Roschini interprets this passage:

Mary stood at the foot of the Cross. Why? To comfort her son? To help him in that dark hour? But she knew she could be of no help to him. Yet she stood, impelled by the duty of offering her Son for the salvation of the world to the extent that it depended on her, just as she had brought him to the light for its salvation to unite her sacrifice to that of her son. She stood on her feet 'stabat', like a priest offering his sacrifice to God for all humanity....One can say of her that she, the earthly mother of Jesus, like his heavenly Father, 'did not spare his own son but gave him up for us!'[7]

In this interpretation, Mary no longer is the heartbroken, sorrowing mother who, driven by maternal instinct watches the cruel death of her Son, but some kind of a supernatural being fulfilling her mission as Co-Redemptress side by side with her Son.

What a distortion of the story of the crucifixion as presented by the synoptic Gospels and by John, where she appears to be stricken with silent grief and speechless, confused and bewildered. In the New Testament Miriam seems to have recovered her spiritual equilibrium only after the resurrection. It was then that she joined the disciples and together with "His brethren" formed a fellowship of faith and worship.

MARY'S CO-REDEEMERSHIP IN TRADITION

As far as the tradition of the early Church is concerned, which, according to Rome, is a second and equally valid source of doctrine, the idea of Mary's co-redeemership is absent. This idea gradually gained ground as an outgrowth of the parallel between Eve and Mary, first mentioned by Irenaeus. However, it is interesting to note that in the letters of Paul there is no reference to Mary at all, and she plays no role in the act of redemption in any of the New Testament writings.

There can be no doubt that sooner or later, the dogma of Mary's Co-Redeemership in association with Christ will be officially defined and will thus become an article of faith.

Judging from the accelerated tempo of mariological development, it should not take the 94 years which it took between the promulgation of the dogma of the Immaculate Conception in 1854 and the dogma of the Assumption in 1950.

Will the future dogma of Mary's Mediatorship lead to further extravagant teachings, such as her "associate membership in the Holy Trinity"?

This is the question which only time will answer.

The dynamics of Marian piety and the peculiar logic of Mariology seem to indicate such a possibility.

The parallel between what the New Testament teaches concerning Jesus and the Roman Church teaches about Mary is remarkable and striking :

Christ was born of a virgin. Mary was immaculately conceived.

Christ was without sin. Mary the Immaculate was without sin.

Christ was the Son of God. Mary the Mother of God.

Christ offered Himself up on the cross. Mary offered up her Son at the Cross.

Christ is our Redeemer. Mary is the Co-Redemptress.

Christ is our Mediator. Mary is the Mediatrix.

Christ sits at the right hand of the Father. Mary sits at the right hand of the Son.

Christ is the head of the church. Mary is the heart of the Church.

The dogmatic cycle of parallelism is not yet completed.

CHAPTER TWENTY-ONE

Marian Piety

Those who have not lived close to devout Roman Catholics can hardly realize the intensity of their devotion to the Virgin Mary or the fervency of their feelings for her whom they call the Mother of God.

Years ago the writer was severely injured in an accident and taken, in a semi-conscious condition, to a Catholic hospital in Poland.

The first thing which struck him was the life-size statue of the Virgin Mary who seemed to preside over the whole ward from her position in the floral shrine. Since the healing of the compound fracture took several months, the writer had much time to watch the statue and to listen to the litanies addressed to her in daily devotions:

Holy Mother of God, pray for us.
Mother of our Creator, pray for us.
Virgin most powerful, pray for us.
Seat of wisdom, pray for us.
Mystical rose, pray for us.
Tower of ivory, pray for us.
House of gold, pray for us.
Ark of the covenant, pray for us.
Gate of heaven, pray for us.
Morning star, pray for us.
Refuge of sinners, pray for us.
Queen of angels, pray for us.
Queen of patriarchs, pray for us.
Queen of prophets, pray for us.
Queen of apostles, pray for us.
Queen of martyrs, pray for us.
Queen of confessors, pray for us.
Queen of virgins, pray for us.
Queen of saints, pray for us.

Queen conceived without original sin, pray for us.

Queen assumed to heaven, pray for us.

Poor Miriam! What have they done to you? This thought went through the writer's mind. Would you ever have recognized yourself from the litany ascribed to you by these misguided devotees of yours? How your pure and devout Jewish soul would have shuddered at such idol worship! Perhaps at that time, unbeknown to myself, the thought of making a study about the life of the real mother of Jesus was conceived.

One day, after having been in the hospital for three weeks, while my eyes were roaming among the flowers surrounding the shrine, I suddenly discovered a tiny figure of Jesus hidden away amidst the flowers. It had taken me three weeks to make this discovery.

At that moment it dawned on me that what I saw was the epitome of Roman Catholicism.

The huge figure of Mary, which strikes everybody at first glance, and the puny figure of Jesus hidden away amidst the flowers!

Here was the very root of the difference between scriptural Christianity and the Roman Catholic religion. Is it possible for the twain to meet?

New Testament religion is theocentric and Christocentric; Catholicism is in a large measure Mariocentric. Have we overstated the difference? Catholic theologians would answer yes, and perhaps point to the centrality of Christ in the mass, which is the heart of Catholic worship. We refrain here from discussing the other disturbing aspects of the mass. Yet apart from all other considerations the fact remains that, in the devotion and affections of most Catholics, it is Mary and not Jesus who is in the center of their inward shrines, in their hearts.

Every conceivable honor is showered upon the Virgin Mary. She has been named the patron saint of almost every country under the sun. Among her many titles is of course included that of Queen of America.

It is Mary, rather than her son, to whom ascend the prayers and the loving affection of her devotees. She is the Queen who never fails to take care of those who invoke her intervention. Jesus is portrayed as the severe judge who is best approached through His benevolent and indulgent mother. She is the Mediatrix who approaches the mediator, Jesus.

It is the contention of Catholic theologians that greater devotion to Mary leads to greater love for Jesus. But this is only theory. In reality,

Mary, to use a theatrical term, "upstages" Jesus and takes away from Him His place as the only Savior of men.

Ever since Thomas Aquinas, Catholic theology has, at least in theory, differentiated between three degrees of devotion:

Latria—Adoration of God

Dulia—Veneration of Saints

Hyperdulia—Superveneration reserved exclusively for the Virgin Mary

In practice these distinctions are specious and cannot be kept in separate compartments. The heart does not recognize such distinctions. In the hearts of the Catholic people Mary holds a place which is unrivaled by anyone—even Jesus.

Mary's cult is an extremely jealous one and suffers no rivalry.

Axel Munthe, the Swedish physician, in his autobiographic novel, *Memories and Vagaries*, relates his curious experience in an Italian village, during the celebration of one of Mary's feast days. (There are 17 feast days devoted to Mary in the Catholic calendar.) The festively dressed statue of the Virgin was carried through the village and the people were having a high time.

When Axel Munthe asked one of the peasants why all these jollities and why Jesus had no place in it, he was told that Jesus was merely a minor saint who would have been completely unknown if he had not had the good fortune to be born of the virgin Mary.

Does this viewpoint strike us as comical? Of course it does. Nevertheless this reflects the psychological and emotional attitude of the Catholic masses to the respective positions of Jesus and Mary. This is Marianity at the grass roots level.

Catholic theology is extremely sensitive to the structural weaknesses of Mariology. This is evident from their constant efforts to defend the Marian dogmas.

Thus Herman Volk, the German Mariologist makes these significant and revealing observations (author's translation) :

Whereas Evangelical Christendom is united in the thought: Christ the hope of the world (compare 1 Timothy 1:1), Catholic Christendom seems today to be more or less united in the thought: Mary the Hope of the World.

*It cannot be disputed that the burden of proof lies on our side, the
burden of proof that this hope which Catholic Christendom puts in
Mary does not question the uniqueness, the once-for-all character
and totality of Christ; that the adoration of Mary does not infringe
upon the honor of Christ; that Mary is not the final goal itself;
that she does not have a Christ-opposing, independent status beside
Christ; that on the contrary, the correct thought of Mary leads to
Christ, and that Christ Himself through Mary can become effective
in us.*

*For our own sake and for the sake of the other Christians we are
obliged to explain and give account of the foundation of the adoration of Mary within Catholicism, how this is possible and why
Christ is not thereby obscured.*

*Only when we can accomplish this in a convincing manner that
our adoration of Mary does not detract from Christ, can we, in
view of the scope of Marianity, effectively prevent from making it
more difficult for Protestants than it is necessary, to recognize that
the Catholic church is the Church of Christ and of the Apostles.*

*To speak about Mary in such a fashion that Christ pales into insig-
nificance is just as destructive as it is un-Catholic and un-Marian.*

*Our task therefore is to justify the intensified Marianity of our time
in an integrated relationship to Christ.*[1]

This is well put; the diagnosis is correct. However it must be apparent to the informed student of Christian thought that Volk's task "to
justify the intensified Marianity of our time" is an impossible one. He
rightly says that "Evangelical Christendom is united in the thought:
Christ the Hope of the World, Catholic Christendom in the thought:
Mary the Hope of the World." How can any forced biblical exegesis
or contrived theological argument alter this fact?

Marian piety and dogmatism have an inherent dynamic which is
diametrically opposed to a Christocentric theology. The roots of Marian
piety are not in the New Testament but in the mystery religions of the

antique world and in the popular devotion of baptized pagans.

THE INFLUENCE OF MEDIEVAL CHIVALRY ON DEVOTION TO MARY

It is now generally recognized that the feudal system of the Middle Ages and the institution of knighthood were favorable to the growth of Marian devotion.

Among the responsibilities of every knight was the duty, at least in theory, to protect the widows and orphans and to defend the honor of womanhood. What better object of chivalry could there be than the virgin Mother of God? She was the Madonna—the Lady par excellence, the Queen of every knightly heart.

The veneration of Mary was especially widespread among the various orders of knighthood during the Crusades.

The feudal system of medieval society also favored devotion to Mary. Just as every knight owed allegiance to his patron and lord, who in turn was subject to his prince or king, so by analogy it was easy to imagine a similar ladder of a heavenly hierarchy. Rung by rung the ladder led from the saints to Mary, from Mary to Jesus, from the Son of God to God the Father. The masses even believed, and many still do, that Mary is a short-cut to heaven.

The idea of reaching God through the "proper channels" is still strongly ingrained in popular Catholic thinking even today. Have you ever heard the argument: "If you wanted to reach the president, wouldn't you first try to reach his mother or his wife?"?

THE PSYCHOLOGY OF MARIAN PIETY

In addition to the historical background of Marianity there are strong psychological factors which were of the utmost importance in the development of Marian piety. One of these psychological aspects is rooted in the repressed sex instincts of medieval monastic society. In the image of the perfectly pure and eternally virgin Mother of God, these instincts found their sublimation and ideal personification.

Perhaps the most important element in the cult of Mary is the mother complex which is dormant in the human psyche.

Somewhere in the deep recesses of the human soul there is the little boy or girl who feels guilty and insecure. God may seem far away in the heavens and may represent the stern father image who demands strict compliance with His law. But mother, she is different. She caresses and is indulgent regardless of one's moral or spiritual condition. She is always there to wipe away the tears and to say, "There, there, don't be afraid. I won't let daddy spank you."

The cult of Mary is the "gray market" of Christian devotion. It replaces the need of true repentance, and of a new spiritual rebirth, with a spurious, amoral devotion to an indulgent Mother. It minimizes or even voids the all-availing work of redemption completed by Christ on Calvary, once and for all, and substitutes for it a morally reprehensible cult of the Mother of All Mercies.

Probably the most prominent promoter of Marian piety in modern times was Alfonso Maria de Liguori (1696-1787). His work, *The Glories of Mary*, published in 1750 is the classic handbook of Marian devotion. Alfonso of Liguori declares that Mary's maternal compassion is so boundless that no sinner, however great, is lost who puts himself under her protection. She opens the bottomless pit of God's mercy to whom she wills.

Her powers are without limit. For instance, once there was a magpie who learned to say "Hail Mary." She said it when a hawk was carrying her away and the hawk dropped dead.

One *Ave Maria* is powerful enough to deliver sinners from the snares of the devil, even when said without devotion, even when recited by an adulterous woman. Prayer to Mary is effective *ex opere*—automatically, mechanically. Mary is too compassionate to let anyone perish. One sigh from Mary is more powerful than the prayers of all the saints put together. Even the blood of Christ does not apply to sinners unless Mary commends them to God.

She is a surer ladder to God than Christ.

This dependence upon Mary's mercy has helped to shape the image of Jesus as the severe judge, who, if it were not for the intercession of His mother, would be difficult to approach.

Such a view of Jesus is reflected in many of the prayers directed to Mary. Here is a typical prayer:

> *O Mother of perpetual help! Thou art the dispenser of all the gifts which God grants to us, miserable sinners; and for this end he has made thee so powerful, so rich and so bountiful, in order that thou*

mayest succour us in our misery.

Thou art the advocate of the most wretched and abandoned sinners who have recourse to thee; come to my help; I commend myself to thee. In thy hands I place my eternal salvation, and to thee I intrust my soul.

Count me among thy most devoted servants; take me under thy protection, and it is enough for me. For, if thou protect me, I fear nothing; not from my sins, because thou wilt obtain for me the pardon of them; nor from the devils, because thou art more powerful than all hell together; nor even from Jesus, my Judge, because by one prayer from thee he will be appeased. But one thing I fear; that in the hour of temptation, I may, through negligence, fail to have recourse to thee, and thus perish miserably.

Obtain for me, therefore, the pardon of my sins, love for Jesus, final perseverance, and the grace ever to have recourse to thee, O mother of perpetual help! [2]

The view of Jesus as the condemning judge rather than Savior can in no way be reconciled with the words of Christ Himself: "Him that cometh to me I will in no wise cast out" (Jn. 6:37).

Nor can it be reconciled with His invitation to all men: "Come unto me all ye that labor and are heavy laden, and I will give you rest" (Mt. 11:28).

The "Come unto me" does not include Mary, in spite of all adroit manipulations with the Scriptures.

Contrary to all mariological subtleties, the statement "I will give you rest" refers only to Christ and not to Mary also.

This forceful interposition of Mary into the mediatorship of Jesus is the point where Catholicism takes leave of the historical Christian *kerygma* that Christ is the all-sufficient Savior of men.

Yet there is something tender and humanly understandable in the devotion to Mary. It is the reaching out of the child for the comforting arms of its mother. But by the same token Marian piety is an unintentional confession that Christ is not the all-sufficient Savior, and that an additional Co-Redemptress is necessary to complete salvation or to make it more accessible to men.

The ever growing image of Mary in Catholic dogma and devotion bears witness that the image of Christ has, in the course of the centuries, faded away, and that it had to be replaced or reinforced with the image of an exalted feminine being who is closely associated with the Trinity.

Has the tidal wave of Marian piety driven Catholicism beyond the point of return?

This is a question which concerns deeply all Christians who are burdened for the integrity of the Gospel message and the unity of the church of Christ.

In spite of recent efforts made by the Pope to bring about a rapprochement between Rome and "the separated brethren," Marianity is driving deeper the wedge between scripturally-oriented Christendom and Roman Catholicism.[3] This is the tragedy of the Marian cult.

Humanly speaking, the prospect for the reconciliation between these two opposite poles of Christianity does not appear to be promising.

However, with God all things are possible, even the return of the ancient Church of Rome to the authentic New Testament position and to its pristine truth. To this end Christians need to pray together with her divine Savior:

That they all may be one as thou, Father, art in me, and I in thee
that they also may be one in us: that the world may believe that
thou hast sent me (Jn. 17:21).

Miriam in the Talmud

It was natural that the mother of Jesus should stir the imagination and arouse the curiosity of many people, both among Christians and non-Christians. Consequently we find numerous references to Miriam in post-biblical literature. Most of these references, as we would expect, were connected with some phase in the life of Jesus. In addition to the various stories and legends about Miriam in the New Testament Apocrypha, which we have already mentioned on previous occasions, we find a number of references to her in the following writings:

1. The Talmud and later rabbinic sources
2. The Qur'an
3. Patristic and sectarian literature

The talmudical references to Miriam and to Jesus are mainly of a derogatory character. The increasingly hostile controversy between Jews and Christians has affected every mention of Jesus and of His mother. Thus Jesus is referred to as *Mamzer ben niddah;*—the illegitimate son of a woman in her separation."[1]

In order to understand properly the talmudical references or cryptic allusions to Miriam and Jesus, it is necessary to bear in mind the religious and political climate of those times.

At the time when the Talmud was committed to writing and compiled in its present form (towards the end of the sixth century AD), Christianity had already become the dominant religion of the Roman Empire. By this time, the church had already shown her growing hostility to the Jews who were frequently taunted as "Christ-killers." The only way Jews could retaliate against their opponents was by denouncing or ridiculing Jesus, whom they had come to consider as the fountainhead of their troubles.

However, this desire to "get even" is only a part of the picture. The religious leaders of Judaism, having once committed themselves to the rejection of Jesus, to be consistent, had to continue to denounce Him in order to justify their negative attitude toward Him to the succeeding generations of Jews, and to portray Him as "a blasphemer and seducer of Israel." Their hostility to Jesus was extended to His mother and to His Jewish disciples.

Already toward the end of the first century, to the solemn prayer, repeated three times daily, *Shmonei Esrei* (The 18 Benedictions) a "benediction" or rather "male-diction" against Hebrew Christians was added.[2] This had the effect of separating and forcing Jewish Christians out of the Temple and synagogue, where apparently they first worshiped together with their people (Acts 2:46).

The relationship between Hebrew Christians and rabbinical Judaism became even more exacerbated during the times of the famous Bar Kochba (or Bar Koziba), who in AD 133, led a disastrous revolt against Roman rule in Palestine. His great admirer and pillar of traditional Judaism, Rabbi Akiba Ben Meir, proclaimed Bar Koziba as the messiah of Israel and nicknamed him *Bar Kochba*—The Son of the Star. This was an allusion to the prophecy of Numbers 24:17: "There shall come a Star out of Jacob, and a Sceptre shall rise out of Israel."

Obviously, Jews who believed Jesus to be the true Messiah could not lend their support to a pseudo-messiah. As Christians they also felt a natural inhibition to use violence or to engage in military measures in order to gain political ends. It was at that time that Jewish Christians were compelled to make their final exit from Palestine and the life of the synagogue. Many of them settled in Pella across the Jordan and became known as the Ebionites, or the Poor Ones.[3]

With the passing of time, the nature and the chronological sequence of events in the life of Jesus became obscured, so that the times of Jesus were confused by some of the talmudical teachers with those of His chief opponent, Rabbi Akiba, who lived about a century later than Jesus. The Talmud also identified the city of Lydda, the place where Rabbi Akiba lived with the place where Jesus lived and was put to death.[4]

Generally speaking, neither the Talmud nor the Qur'an show any deep concern for historical accuracy. Anachronisms relating to early Christianity are fairly common in both. On the whole it is remarkable how few references to Jesus there are in the Talmud. This was probably due to the fact that after the destruction of the Temple in AD 70, the main advance of the church was in the north, in Asia Minor, in the west, in Europe, and southwest, in Africa. The rapid expansion of the church largely bypassed the two main centers of Jewish religious life, which was in Palestine and in Babylon, the seats of the great talmudical schools.

What references to Miriam, to Jesus, or to His disciples there are in the Talmud, were based on half-forgotten traditions and legends which caricatured events related in the Gospels.

When later, during the Middle Ages, the Church became the dominant religious and political power in the West, she forced the expurgation from the Talmud of all passages which were considered to be of an anti-Christian character. Sometimes the Talmud and other rabbinical writings were either confiscated or ordered to be burned. In this respect the church has shown the way to Hitler and to his henchmen, who ordered the burning of Jewish and other writings which were not to his liking.[5]

One feels rather embarrassed to quote some of the talmudical references to Jesus or to Miriam. The modern reader, Jew or Gentile, is bound to feel an aversion to them. Yet since we have committed ourselves to the task of presenting the person of Miriam in the Bible, and in postbiblical tradition, it is necessary to complete the picture.

Just one word of warning to the reader. It would be most unfair to saddle any contemporary Jew with the ancient opinions held during the heat of a running dispute by some of his forefathers some 15 to 18 centuries ago. Today many Jews look upon Jesus as great man, or even as the greatest of their prophets and teachers, even if they deny His Messianic claims.

SON OF STADA AND SON OF PANDERA

We come now to consider some of the talmudical references to Jesus and His mother.

In the Talmud and in later rabbinical literature, Jesus is commonly referred to as Son of Stada or Son of Pandera. In the Jerusalem Talmud Aboda Zara 2,40d He is called *Jeshu ben Pandera,* and in Jerusalem Talmud Sabbath 14,14d, briefly *Jeshu Pandera.* In two almost identical passages, Shabbath 104b and Sanhedrin 67a, we read:

The son of Stada was the son of Pandera. Rab Chisda said: The

husband was Stada, the lover Pandera. (Another said) The Hus-
band was Paphos ben Jehudah; Stada was his mother; (or) his
mother was Miriam, the women's hairdresser; as they would say at
Pumbeditha s'tath da (i.e., she was unfaithful) to her husband.

In more intelligible language, with the needful additions, which are
so constantly lacking in the Talmud by reason of its conciseness, the
passage runs thus:

He (Jesus) was not the son of Stada, but he was the son of Pandera.
Rab Chisda said: The husband of Jesus' mother was Stada, but her
lover was Pandera. Another said: Her husband was surely Paphos
ben Jehudah; on the contrary Stada was his mother; or, accord-
ing to others his mother was Miriam, the women's hairdresser.
The rejoinder is: Quite so, but Stada is her nickname, as it is said
at Pumbeditha, S'tath da (she proved faithless) to her husband.[6]
["Miriam the Hairdresser"—in Hebrew, Miriam Megaddla—
apparently rests on a confusion of the mother of Jesus with Mary
Magdalene.]

The above passages date from the beginning of the fourth century.
We know that Rabbi Chisda, mentioned in this passage, died in AD 309.
Stada, according to the Talmud, is a woman who has been unfaithful
to her husband, thus making Jesus the illegitimate son of an unfaithful
woman.

There is also the possibilit y that the word *Sathda* or *Satra* is a cor-
ruption of the Greek word *soter*—savior.

As for the name *Pandera* or *Pantera*, it probably stands for the Greek
word *panther*. Ben Pandra or Panthera would therefore mean the son
of Panther, meaning the son of sensuality. Panther was the symbol of
lewdness. Pandera may also have been a play of words on the Greek
Parthenos. Since the Christians referred to Jesus as the Son of a Virgin
(*Parthenos*), so they nicknamed Him the Son of Panthera.

In Gittin 90a there is the following rather cryptic reference to Miriam
and her husband, called there Paphos ben Jehudah:

There is a tradition, R. Meir used to say: Just as there are various kinds of taste as regards eating, so there are also various dispositions as regards women. There is a man into whose cup a fly falls and he casts it out, but all the same he does not drink it (the cup). Such was the manner of Paphos ben Jehudah, who used to lock the door upon his wife, and go out.

The sense of this reference is this: Miriam's husband Paphos (Joseph) suspecting his wife of unfaithfulness used to lock her up whenever he left home. She, however, broke loose, lived unchastely, and out of such a connection Jesus was born, of one habitually unfaithful.

The talmudical allusions to Miriam were by no means consistent, but represent a variety of traditions. In Sanhedrin 106a we read: "She (Miriam) who was the descendant of princes and governors, played the harlot with carpenters." (One text reads: "with a carpenter.")

This reference is of special interest as it indicates that there was a tradition among the Jews that Miriam was of princely descent.

There are a number of similar references of a distasteful character in the Talmud which we will not quote.[7]

Unfortunately, G. Dalman's and Heinrich Laible's study (translated by A. W. Streane), *Jesus Christ in the Talmud,* published in 1893, is now out of print. There all the references to Miriam and Jesus in the Talmud and in later rabbinical literature are quoted verbatim from the original, translated into English and discussed in detail. Since our study is concerned primarily with the person of Miriam and only incidentally with Jesus we shall omit most of the passages in the Talmud which refer to Him.

In recent times, under the impact of persecutions, or for fear of anti-Semitism in so-called Christian countries there has been a tendency among some rabbinical scholars to disavow most of the talmudical references as not really referring to Jesus, but to some other persons.[8]

On the basis of such hostile allusions and fables in talmudical literature and oral traditions, a scurrilous story of the life of Jesus in the Hebrew language came into being during the Middle Ages called *Toldoth Jeshu*—The Story of Jesus. The origin of this unsavory pamphlet goes back to the eighth century or even earlier.

The gist of this story is as follows:

*In the days of King Jannaeus (about 90 BC) a misfortune befell the
Jews. A certain man of evil repute by the name of Joseph Pandera
who lived in Bethlehem, seduced a chaste maiden by the name of
Miriam. Out of this illicit connection was born a child named
Jeshu. Because of the impudent demeanor of the boy against the
sages of Israel, his illegitimate origin became known to them and
Jeshu had to flee to Upper Galilee. He later learned the Ineffable
Name of God, the sacred Tetragramaton YHWH (the sacred name
of JEHOVAH), and through this knowledge performed miracles.
He gathered to himself 310 young men and proclaimed himself as
the Messiah. He was eventually captured in Lydda and sentenced
to death. A herald went forth calling witnesses to come forward
and speak in favor of Jeshu, but none came. Jeshu was put to death
on the sixth hour on the eve of Passover and of the Sabbath.*

*On the first day of the week his disciples came to Queen Helen
(Salome Alexandra , executed by Herod the Great for alleged
intrigues against himself about 15 BC). They said that "Jeshu" rose
from the dead. However, the sages of Israel procured his body and
showed it to the queen.*

*For thirty years after this there was a bitter dispute among the
Jews. The followers of Jesus maintained: "You have slain the
Messiah." Their opponents answered: "You have followed a false
prophet."*

*In order to separate the Jewish believers in Jeshu from their people,
the sages of Israel found a man by the name of Simon Kepha,
whom they taught the Ineffable Name. This enabled him to perform
miracles, and to persuade the Jewish Christians that Simon was a
believer in Jeshu.*

*Simon induced the Christians to separate themselves from the
Jews and to observe Sunday instead of Saturday, the Resurrection
instead of the Passover, and to disregard the dietary laws. Thus the
sages of Israel were able to separate the Jewish followers of Jesus
from the rest of the Jews.*

Until comparatively recent times, this medieval travesty, which caricatured the Gospel narrative, was the chief source of information for Jewish people about Jesus. It still lingers on as a kind of folktale among some Jews. However, *Toldoth Jeshu* is today mostly forgotten. Modern Jewish scholars and men of letters like the late Prof. Joseph Klausner of the Hebrew University and the famous novelist Sholem Asch, and many others, have based their works concerning Christ and early Christianity on a thorough study of the New Testament. Most Jewish scholars have denounced *Toldoth Jeshu* as an unworthy product of medieval minds.

Distasteful as the talmudical and later rabbinical references to Jesus may be to the Christian, they also have their positive value, long recognized by scholars. These references confirm the historicity of Jesus and of His mother, Miriam, and also the fact that He was able to perform miracles. This is of special significance because it comes to us out of the mouths of those very people who were most strongly opposed to Him. Thus even "the wrath of man shall praise Him" (Ps. 76:10).

Miriam in the Qur'an

In the Islamic scriptures known as the Qur'an, Jesus is referred to as "Jesus the son of Mary." The statements of the Qur'an about Mary and Jesus obviously reflect to a considerable degree the beliefs of those Christians and Jews with whom Muhammad came into contact during his extensive travels in Arabia and Syria.

What the Qur'an has to say concerning Christians and Jews is important because, for centuries, this has strongly influenced the thinking of the Muslim world and has had a great impact on past and contemporary history.

Much of the Qur'an is a running dispute between Muhammad on the one hand, and Judaism and Christianity on the other.

Before going further, it is well to take a look at the Qur'an, the bible of some 250 million Muslims, and also at the man behind the book.

Around the year AD 570, a man by the name of Muhammad, son of Abdullah, was born in the ancient city of Mecca, in Arabia. This city was an important center of commerce and of Arab worship. According to Arab tradition, Abraham built there a temple called the Ka'bah, dedicated to the only and true God, Allah. This shrine is still considered the most sacred place of the Moslem world. Every faithful Muslim believes it to be his sacred duty to make a pilgrimage to Mecca at least once in a lifetime, more often if possible.

Early in his life young Muhammad was apprenticed to a wealthy widow, who was engaged in a caravan trade between Mecca and Syria. Young Muhammad acquitted himself so well that he soon married this widow, who was 15 years his senior.

During the summer heat it was customary for Muhammad to spend some time near Mt. Hira, in the vicinity of Mecca. It was there that one night he heard a voice which commanded him to "read." Being an illiterate man, Muhammad was astounded.

However, the "voice" insisted three times that he "read." According to Muhammad this was the voice of the angel Gabriel (whom he identified with the Holy Spirit). The angel appeared to him over a period of time and revealed to him messages from God. These revelations Muhammad called the *Qur'an* which means "reading," that is, the reading (or lecture) of the man who did not know how to read.

In his travels through the Arab world Muhammad became well acquainted with Jews, many of whom escaped after the destruction of the Temple in AD 70 to Arabia. There they formed a number of strong, warlike tribes. He also came in close touch with Arab Christians, most of whom belonged to the Jacobite community (the Eastern branch of the church), or to the various Christian sects which at that time proliferated in Arabia. Many of these sectarians were forced to flee from the persecution of Constantine the Great, when he became a Christian early in the fourth century.

Muhammad's knowledge of the Old and New Testaments, as well as of the Talmud and Jewish traditions, was based mainly on these personal contacts with Jews and Christians, whom he called the People of the Book or People of the Scriptures. This knowledge, often distorted and inaccurate, is reflected in the Qur'an. He claimed that the Jews and the Christians, after receiving the Scriptures, distorted them in order to promote their own ideas and to hide the fact that he, Muhammad, was the prophet foretold of God in the Old Testament and also in the New. (He apparently believed himself to be the Comforter whom Christ foretold He would send.) The heart of his message was: "There is no God but Allah, and Muhammad is his prophet."

After his first visions (later written down by his friends and followers), Muhammad returned to Mecca and converted his wife and a few relatives. However, his own kinsmen, the tribe of Qureysh, rejected his claims and his teachings. He also had little success with the Jewish tribes, in spite of his claim that he came to reestablish the pure faith of Abraham, and even ordered his followers to bow toward Jerusalem.

When the Jews refused to receive him as the prophet, he became embittered against them and announced that he had received a later revelation directing the true followers of the prophet Muhammad that they should henceforth bow (the *Kib'la*) towards Mecca and not Jerusalem. This change of direction was of great importance for the relations between the followers of Muhammad and the Jews. It signified a complete breach with Judaism. During the first 13 years of his labors, Muhammad attracted a small following and much persecution from his kinsmen allied with numerous and warlike Jewish tribes.

On the night of June 20, 622, an assassination plot against Muhammad was arranged by some of his fellow citizens of Mecca. However, Muhammad received word of it and escaped. This event became the pivotal experience in Muhammad's life. All events in Muhammad's life and in later Islamic history were henceforth reckoned as either so many years before this escape, known as the *Hijrah,* or after that. Mohammed lived 10 years after the Hijrah, no longer as a traveling teacher of the new religion of Islam (which means "Surrender to God"), but as the increasingly successful ruler of the newly founded Islamic empire which he governed from the city of Medinah.

He died at the age of 63 in the year 632. According to Islamic tradition his death was partly the result of poison administered to him by a woman, some 10 years before.

The Qur'an is composed of 114 *Surahs* or chapters which are of different lengths. Each Surah represents a separate revelation. For the purpose of our study we quote some passages which illustrate Muhammad's attitude toward Christianity and which establish what he believed about Miriam and Jesus.

Many of his thoughts concerning Christ and His mother, Miriam, are expressed in Surah 3, entitled "The Family of Imram": (Amram was the father of Moses and his sister Miriam in the Old Testament, but in the Qur'an, Amram is the father of Miriam or Mary, the mother of Jesus).

And when the angels said: O Mary! Lo! Allah hath chosen thee and made thee pure, and hath preferred thee above (all) the women of creation.

O Mary! Be obedient to thy Lord, prostrate thyself and bow with those who bow (in worship).

This is of the tidings of things hidden. We reveal it unto thee (Muhammad). Thou wast not present with them when they threw their pens (to know) which of them should be the guardian of Mary, nor wast thou present with them when they quarrelled (thereupon).

(And remember) when the angels said: O Mary! Lo! Allah giveth thee glad tidings of a word from Him, whose name is the Messiah Jesus, son of Mary, illustrious in the world and the Hereafter, and one of those brought near (unto Allah).

He will speak unto mankind in his cradle and in his manhood, and he is of the righteous.

She said: My Lord! How can I have a child when no mortal hath touched me? He said: So (it will be), Allah createth what He will. If He decreeth a thing, He saith unto it only: Be! and it is.

And He will teach him the Scripture and wisdom, and the Torah and the Gospel.

And will make him a messenger unto the children of Israel (saying): Lo! I come unto you with a sign from your Lord. Lo! I fashion for you out of clay the likeness of a bird, and I breathe into it and it is a bird, by Allah's leave. I heal him who was born blind, and the leper, and I raise the dead, by Allah's leave. And I announce unto you what ye eat and what ye store up in your houses. Lo! herein verily is a portent for you, if ye are to be believers.

And (I come) confirming that which was before me of the Torah, and to make lawful some of that which was forbidden unto you. I come unto you with a sign from your Lord, so keep your duty to Allah and obey me.

Lo! Allah is my Lord and your Lord, so worship Him. That is a straight path.

But when Jesus became conscious of their disbelief, he cried: Who will be my helpers in the cause of Allah? The disciples said: We will be Allah's helpers. We believe in Allah, and bear thou witness that we have surrendered (unto Him).

Our Lord! We believe that which Thou hast revealed and we follow him whom Thou hast sent. Enroll us among those who witness (to the truth).

And they (the disbelievers) schemed, and Allah schemed (against them): and Allah is the best of schemers.

(And remember) when Allah said: O Jesus! Lo! I am gathering thee and causing thee to ascend unto Me, and am cleansing thee of those who disbelieve and am setting those who follow thee above those who disbelieve until the Day of Resurrection. Then unto Me ye will (all) return, and I shall judge between you as to that wherein ye used to differ.

As for those who disbelieve I shall chastise them with a heavy chastisement in the world and the Hereafter; and they will have no helpers.

And as for those who believe and do good works, He will pay them their wages in full. Allah loveth not wrongdoers.

This (which) we recite unto thee is a revelation and a wise reminder.

Lo! The likeness of Jesus with Allah is as the likeness of Adam. He created him of dust, then he said unto him: Be! And he is.

(This is) the truth from thy Lord (O Muhammad), so be not thou of those who waver.

And who disputeth with thee concerning him, after the knowledge which hath come unto thee, say (unto him); Come! We will summon our sons and your sons, and our women and your women, and ourselves and yourselves, then we will pray humbly (to our Lord) and (solemnly) invoke the curse of Allah upon those who lie.

Lo! This verily is the true narrative. There is no God save Allah, and lo! Allah is the Mighty, the Wise.

And if they turn away, then lo! Allah is aware of (who are) the corrupters.

Say: O People of the Scripture. Come to an agreement between us and you; that we shall worship none but Allah, and that we shall ascribe no partner unto Him, and that none of us shall take others for Lords beside Allah. And if they run away, then say: Bear witness that we are they who have surrendered (unto Him).

O People of the Scripture! Why will ye argue about Abraham, when the Torah and the Gospel were not revealed till after him? Have ye no sense?" (Surah 3:42–65).1

Much of what has been quoted above indicates that Muhammad used both the Gospel narrative as well as extra-canonical traditions and legends such as were preserved in post-New Testament traditions and apocryphal writings. We have already mentioned in chapter 10 of this study that according to some, Miriam was supposed to have been raised in the Temple by the high priest and his associates, until she was 12 years old. After this, lots were cast to decide who should be her guardian. The Qur'an follows this tradition. The fashioning by the boy Jesus of a clay bird, into which He breathed life, again was common legend current in early Christian literature and preserved in the apocryphal Gospel of St. Thomas.

In common with the Jews and some Christian sects, Muhammad strongly denounced the doctrine of the Trinity. This is reflected in the above quotation from the Qur'an.

Gospel events are reflected in the Qur'an as if in a distorted mirror. Muhammad both confirms and denies the Torah and the Gospels.

The story of the annunciation and the birth of Jesus is also related in Surah 19, called "Mary."

There we are told that Miriam conceived of the Holy Spirit, who took on the likeness of a perfect man (Surah 19:17). After her conception she withdrew to a distant place and took shelter in the trunk of a palm tree, the dates of which nourished her.

According to the Qur'an, the name of Mary's brother was Aaron (Surah 19:28). This in addition to the fact that "Imram" or Amram, who is the father of Moses (Ex. 6:20), has led many to be of the opinion that Muhammad was confused as regards chronology and the identity of some biblical personalities.

When Jesus was in the cradle, according to the Qur'an, He spoke and said: "I am a slave of Allah, He hath given me the Scriptures and appointed me a prophet" (Surah19:29–30). This is a tradition derived from the numerous Infancy Gospels.

Again, Muhammad strongly denounced the doctrine of the Triune God in the following words:

"They surely disbelieve who say: Allah is the Messiah, son of Mary. The surely disbelieved who say: Allah is the third of three" (Surah 5:72–73).

"The Messiah, son of Mary, was no other than a messenger, messengers (the like of whom) have passed away before him. And his mother was a saintly woman" (Surah 5:75).

However, the idea of the Trinity which Muhammad received from some Christians was that Mary was one person of the Trinity.

And when Allah saith: O Jesus, son of Mary! Didst thou say unto mankind: Take me and my mother for two gods beside Allah? he saith: Be glorified! It was not mine to utter that to which I had no right. I spake unto them only that which Thou commendedst me (Surah 5:116–117).

Eusebius in his *Ecclesiastical History* states that at the Council of Nice, in AD 325, there was a sect known as the Miriamites, who believed that Mary or Miriam was one of the persons of the holy Trinity.[2]

Obviously, by the seventh century the cult of Mary had become so widespread and deep-rooted that Muhammad was led to think that according to Christian doctrine Mary, Jesus, and God the Father formed a Trinity.

Those who have followed the progressive trend toward the deification of Mary in Marian theology can readily sympathize with Muhammad and understand why he made such a mistake.

Theoretically the Qur'an recognizes the Scriptures of the Old and the New Testament (of which it is claimed there were 104 books). Special recognition is given to the Pentateuch, the book of Psalms, and to the Gospels.[3] However, these books, according to Muhammad, have been tampered with by the Jews and the Christians. Peculiarly, Muhammad seems to think that Ezra the Scribe was worshiped by the Jews as the Son of God, just as the Christians consider Jesus as the Son of God.

Fact and fancy are constantly mixed up in the Qur'an:

And the Jews say: Ezra is the son of Allah, and the Christians say: The Messiah is the son of Allah. That is their saying with their mouths. They imitate the saying of those who disbelieved of old. Allah (Himself) fighteth against them. How perverse are they!

They have taken as lords beside Allah their rabbis and their monks and the Messiah son of Mary, when they were bidden to worship only one God. There is no God save Him. Be He glorified from all that they ascribe as partner (unto Him)! (Surah 9:30–31)

It is apparent that what knowledge Muhammad had of Judaism and Christianity came to him secondhand and often from tainted sources. In the Qur'an the Old and New Testament Scriptures, the Talmud and apocryphal traditions are mixed up together.

Generally, Muhammad shows respect for Miriam as a "saintly woman" and for Jesus as being a great prophet and "one of God's messengers," but denounced His divinity, and what He imagined was the Christian doctrine of the Trinity.

The Deposit of Faith

The Church of Rome claims that it never changes, and always teaches and believes the same doctrines. To explain the obvious fact that dogmas have been introduced into the Church at certain points in history, a convenient fiction has been introduced called The Deposit of Faith. This is the body of revelation contained in Scripture and tradition, supposedly delivered by Christ to His apostles (1 Tim. 6:20).[1] The Deposit of Faith contains those "truths" which the Church has always believed "in seed," but were later defined as articles of faith.

Here are some of the dates when the "unchangeable Church of Rome" introduced certain beliefs and practices:

Prayers for the dead	300
Mary proclaimed "Mother of God"	431
Worship in Latin	600
Supremecy of the Pope	
Boniface takes title of "Universal	
Bishop," thus becoming first pope	606
Veneration of images and relics	788
Holy water introduced	1000
Marriage of priest forbidden	1079
Rosary beads	1090
Confession to the priest	1215
Transubstantiation of wafer	1215
Adoration of wafer	1220
Purgatory proclaimed	1439
Apocryphal books added to the Bible	1546
Tradition made of equal force	
with the Bible (Deposit of Faith)	1546
Immaculate Conception of Mary	1854

Infallibility of the Pope   1870
The Assumption of Mary 1950^{2}

NOTES

INTRODUCTION

1 Roschini Mariologia I, 63, quoted by Giovanni Miegge in *The Virgin Mary*, 50.

2 A similar division is mentioned in Luke 24:44, "which were written in the law of Moses, and in the prophets, and in the psalms." The Psalms were first in the section called *The Writings*.

3 See article "Bible Canon" in *The Jewish Encyclopedia*, Vol. 3.

4 "For alms delivereth from death, and the same is that which purgeth away sins, and maketh to find mercy and life everlasting" (Tobit 12:9).

5 "And making a gathering, he sent twelve thousand drachms of silver to Jerusalem for sacrifice to be offered for the sins of the dead, thinking well and religiously concerning the resurrection, (for if he had not hoped that they that were slain should rise again, it would have seemed superfluous and vain to pray for the dead,) and because he considered that they who had fallen asleep with godliness, had great grace laid up for them. It is therefore a holy and wholesome thought to pray for the dead, that they may be loosed from sins" (2 Macc. 12:43–46).

6 *The Life,* Josephus' autobiography, and other works by Josephus.

7 *The Dead Sea Scrolls,* by Millar Burrows.
The Dead Sea Scriptures, translated by Theodore H. Gaster.

8 Miriam, the mother of Jesus is called the daughter of Amram, who was the father of Moses and of his sister Miriam. The Qur'an seems to confuse the two Miriams.

9 For a full discussion of the references and allusions to Jesus and Miriam in the Talmud, we refer to Gustaf Dalman's *Jesus Christ in the Talmud.*

10 *The Messianic Idea in Israel,* by Joseph Klausner.

CHAPTER 1: THE POLITICAL BACKGROUND

1 Cyrus Cylinder, 24-33, quoted by W. S. LaSor in *Great Personalities of the Old Testament*, 177.

2 For details of this struggle, see Victor Buksbazen's *The Gospel in the Feasts of Israel*, chapter 7.

3 Josephus, Flavius: "So furious was he (Alexander Jannsus, 104-78 BC,

son of John Hyrcanus, the Hasmonean) that his savagery went to
the length of impiety. He had eight hundred of his captives (all Jews)
crucified in the midst of the city (in Jerusalem), and their wives and
children butchered before their eyes, while he looked on, drinking, with
his concubines."—*Jewish War* Book I, 96-101 (Ant. XIII, 380-391),
(Thackeray, 49).

4   Josephus, Flavius, *Antiquities*, Book 16, chap. 5.

CHAPTER 2: GALILEE IN THE DAYS OF CHRIST

1   *Jewish War III,* Josephus, 40-43, H. St. J. Thackeray.

2   *Sketches of Jewish Life,* Alfred Edersheim, 30.

3   Edersheim, Op. cit., 36.

4   "But of the fourth sect of Jewish philosophy, Judas the Galilean was the
author. These men agree in all other things with the Pharisaic notions:
but they have an inviolable attachment to Liberty; and say that God is
to be their only Ruler and Lord.
"They also do not value dying any kinds of death, nor indeed do
they heed the deaths of their relations and friends, nor can any such
fear make them call any man Lord.... It was in Gessius Florus's time
(approximately AD 66) that the nation began to grow mad with this
distemper, who was our procurator, and who occasioned the Jews to go
wild with it by the abuse of his authority, and to make them revolt from
the Romans"—*Antiquities,* Josephus, Book 18, chap. 1, sec. 6, William
Whiston, trans.

5   It is reported that the famous R. Johanan be Zakkai, provoked by the
neglect of the Galileans to profit by his presence and teaching, said: "O
Galilee, Galilee, thou hatest the Law; thine end will be to have to deal
with robbers"—Jerusalem Shabbat 15d, quoted in *Judaism in the First
Centuries of the Christian Era,* George Foot Moore, Vol. III, 35.
See also *The Pharisees,* Louis Finkelstein, Vol. 1, 52.

6   "Galileans are censured for their slovenly pronunciation in general
('Erubin 53a)—they pronounced "hlb" so that you could not tell
whether they said "milk" (*halab*), or "suet" (*heleb*, prohibited) it was that
you were invited to eat, and particularly ridiculed their confusion of the
gutterals—when a Galilean said "amar," nobody could tell whether he
meant an "ass" (*hamor*), or "wine" (*hamar*) or "wool" ('amar), or a "lamb"
(*aimar*). Erubin 53b, George Foot Moore, Op. cit., Vol. III, 160–161.

7   Edersheim, Op. cit., 224.

8   Berachoth 6a, quoted in *Sketches of Jewish Life,* Edersheim, 222.

9   *Antiquities,* Josephus, Book 17, chap. 2, sec. 4.

10 Edersheim, Op. cit., 236.

11 Edersheim, Op. cit., 215 and following.

12 "Then come unto him, the Sadducees, which say there is no resurrection" (Mk. 12:18)."For the Sadducees say that there is no resurrection, neither angel, nor spirit: but the Pharisees confess both" (Acts 23:8).

13 "The doctrine of the Essens is this: That all things are best ascribed to God. They teach the immortality of souls, and esteem that the rewards of righteousness are to be earnestly striven for; and when they send what they have dedicated to God into the temple, they do not offer sacrifices, because they have more pure lustrations of their own; on which account they are excluded from the common court of the temple, but offer their sacrifices themselves yet is their course of life better than that of other men; and they entirely addict themselves to husbandry. It also deserves our admiration, how much they exceed all other men that addict themselves to virtue, and this in righteousness:

This is demonstrated by that institution of theirs, which will not suffer any thing to hinder them from having all things in common; so that a rich man enjoys no more of his own wealth than he who hath nothing at all.

"There are about four thousand men that live in this way, and neither marry wives, nor are desirous to keep servants; as thinking the latter tempts men to be unjust, and the former gives the handle to domestic quarrels; but as they live by themselves, they minister one to another"— *Antiquities,* Josephus, Book 18, chap. l, sec. 5.See also "The Community of Qumran," article in *The Bridge,* Vol. II, John M. Oesterreicher, ed.

CHAPTER 3: WOMAN IN JEWISH LIFE

1   *The Wisdom of Ben-Sira,* chap. 24:1–4.

2   Ibid., chap. 25:18–19, 23.

3   Shabbath 23, quoted by Edersheim in *Sketches of Jewish Life,* 140.

4   C. G. Montefiore, *Rabbinic Literature and Gospel Teachings,*47.

5   Montefiore, Op. cit., 218.

6   G. Lowes Dickinson, *The Greek View of Life,*169.

[7] Dickinson, Op. cit., 175.

[8] Thucydides II, 45.

[9] Dickinson, Op. cit.,176.

[10] Dickinson, Op. cit.,183.

[11] Edith Hamilton, *The Roman Way* (Mentor Edition), 141.

[12] Anne Fremantle, *A Treasury of Early Christianity,*59-60.

[13] S. Singer, *The Standard Prayer Book*, 6.

[14] Berachoth 17a.

[15] Genesis Rabbah 45:2.

[16] Baba Metsia 88b.

[17] Edersheim, *Sketches of Jewish Life,* 206.

CHAPTER 4: MARRIAGE AND FAMILY LIFE

[1] Mishna Kiddushin 1:1, 321 (Herbert Danby, trans).

[2] Kiddushin 2b.

[3] A. Cohen, *Everyman's Talmud,*166.

[4] Ketuboth 8:1.

[5] Ketuboth 1:2.

[6] See also articles on Money and Wages in *Davis Dictionary of the Bible.*

[7] Some time ago public opinion in Israel was shocked by the marriage of Rabbi Toledano, minister of religious affairs, a man of over 80 to a girl of 18, after payment of a suitable *mohar* to her impoverished Moroccan parents. *Illustrierte Welt Woch,* Tel Aviv, July 13, 1960.

[8] Singer, *The Standard Prayer Book,* 443.

[9] Danby, Op. cit., Mishna, Tractate Yebamoth 6:6, 227.

[10] Mishna Ketuboth 7:6.

[11] Danby, Op. cit., Mishna Ketuboth 5:5, 252.

[12] Berachoth 64a.

[13] Berachoth 8b.

[14] Genesis Rabbah 71:6.

[15] Shabboth 127a.

[16] Genesis Rabbath 49:4.

[17] Public schools existed in Sumer as far back as 2500 BC, but they were not compulsory. See S. N. Kramer, *History Begins in Sumer,* Doubleday.

[18] Aboth 5:24.

[19] Baba Metzia 11:11.

[20] Sanhedrin 99a.

21 Chagigah 9b.
22 Leviticus Rabbah 7:3.
23 Baba Kama 8:2b.
24 Mishna, Tractate Sotah 3:4.
25 Sotah 19a.
26 Mishna Sotah 3:4.

CHAPTER 5: NEW TESTAMENT REFERENCES TO MIRIAM

1 C. G. Montefiore and H. Loewe, *A Rabbinic Anthology*, 440-441.
2 *History of Joseph the Carpenter*, chap. 2.
3 Book of James VIII:I--IX:2 in *The Apocryphal New Testament*, M. R. James trans., 42.
4 *The Death of Joseph*, XIV Op. cit., 85.
5 Edersheim, *The Life and Times of Jesus the Messiah*, Vol.1, 156.

CHAPTER 6: THE ANNUNCIATION

1 Werner Keller, *The Bible As History*, 342-343.
2 Book of Enoch 40:6, 54:6.
3 Canticles Rabbah 2: 11.
4 Exodus R. 26:1.
5 Ta'anith 9a.
6 Baba Bathra 17a.
7 Bereshith R. 23, Warsh, ed., 45b quoted by Edersheim, *Life and Times of Jesus the Messiah*, Vol. 1, 177.
8 Bereshith R. 51, ed. Warsh. p. 95a, Op. cit., 178.

CHAPTER 7: MIRIAM AND ELISABETH

1 Rashi (or Rabbi Shlomo Itzchaki) commentary, Genesis 25:22–23.
2 The apocryphal book of Judith 13:18, recognized as part of the Bible by the Church of Rome, but not included in the Old Testament canon by the Jews or Protestants.

CHAPTER 8: THE MAGNIFICAT

1 Some people confuse the non-biblical doctrine of the Immaculate Conception as taught by the Church of Rome with the scriptural teaching concerning the virgin birth of the Messiah (Isa. 7:14; Mt. 1:18, 22–23). Catholic theologians explain the Immaculate Conception as

Mary's complete immunity from original sin. "Even before her birth, God planned to safeguard the mother of His Son, by virtue of His merits, from any taint of original sin." Dr. N. G. M. Van Doornik, et al., *A Handbook of the Catholic Faith*, 238.

The same book, on the same page, blandly admits "This point of doctrine is not expressly dealt with anywhere in the Bible, nor was it preached by the Apostles, and for many centuries it was not mentioned at all by the Church...the view...was formally pronounced as a dogma of the Church by His Holiness Pope Pius IX in 1854."Op. cit., 238.

2 The Talmud records the curse which a distinguished rabbi of Jerusalem, Abba Shaul, pronounced upon the high priestly families who were "themselves High-Priest, their sons treasurers of the Temple, their sons-in-law assistant-treasurers, while their servants beat the people with sticks." Pes. 57a, Edersheim in *Life and Times of Jesus the Messiah*, Vol. 1, 372, eighth revised edition.

CHAPTER 9: THE BIRTH OF JESUS

1 William Ramsay, *The Bearing of Recent Discovery on the Trustworthiness of the New Testament*, 222.
2 Josephus, *Antiquities*, Book 17, chap. 6, paragraph 4.
3 Cornelius Tacitus, *Annals*, XV, 44.
4 Recently a stone was found near Caesarea, the Roman administrative capital of first-century Palestine, bearing the inscription of Tiberius and Pontius Pilate.
5 In the Hebrew and Arabic languages the word for *Christians* is still today "Nazarenes."
6 Edersheim, *Life and Times of Jesus the Messiah*, Vol. 1, 186-187.

CHAPTER 10: THE ANCESTRY OF MIRIAM AND JOSEPH

1 Kid. 69b.
2 Pes. 62b.
3 See Davis' *Dictionary of the Bible* article "Genealogy," 251-53.
4 The *Apocryphal New Testament*, Book of James, 39-43, M. R. James, trans.
5 In English the words *Jesus* and *save* have no apparent relationship, but they are obviously related in the Hebrew language. The Hebrew name *Jeshua* and the word for salvation *Jeshuah* are almost identical (except

for a minor detail in spelling—the soundless "h" at the end). Both stem from the same root *Jeshah,* which means "to save." The name *Jesus* has come to us via several foreign languages. In the original Hebrew the name was *Yeshua,* an abbreviated version of the name *Jehoshua,* "Jehova is salvation."

CHAPTER 11: THE PURIFICATION AND PRESENTATION

1   Strack-Billerbeck, *Kommentar zum Neuen Testament aus Talmud und Midrasch,* Vol. 2, 124-26.

2   In *The War of the Sons of Light and the Sons of Darkness* we find the following expression of hope for Israel's future deliverance and glory: "Arise, O warrior! Take thy captives, thou man of glory; and reap thy spoil, O valiant! Set thy hand upon the neck of the foemen,
And thy foot upon mounds of the slain.
Smite the nations that assail thee, and let thy sword devour guilty flesh.
Fill thy land with glory and Thine inheritance with blessing.
Be a multitude of possessions in Thy fields,
Silver and gold and precious stones in Thy palaces.
Zion, rejoice exceedingly, and shine forth, O Jerusalem, with songs of joy,
And let all the cities of Judah exult! Let thy gates be continually open,
That the wealth of the nations may be brought unto thee; And let their kings minister unto thee,
And all that oppressed thee make obeisance to thee, And lick the dust of thy feet!"
-Theodor H. Caster, *The Dead Sea Scriptures,* 297-298.

3   In one of the "Psalms of Thanksgiving" in the Dead Sea Scrolls, we find the following hymn, so strangely reminiscent of Luke's story of the birth of Jesus:
"Yea, I am in distress as a woman in travail bringing forth her firstborn, when, as her time draws near, the pangs come swiftly upon her and all the grievous throes that rack those heavy with child.
For now, amid throes of death, new life is coming to birth, and the pangs of travail set in, as at last there enters the world the man-child long conceived. Now, amid throes of death, that man-child long foretold is about to be brought forth.
Now, amid pangs of hell there will burst forth from the womb that

marvel of mind and might, and that man-child will spring from the throes!" Caster, Op. cit., 135–136.

CHAPTER 12: BETWEEN BOYHOOD AND MANHOOD

1 *Israel My Glory,* December 1961/January 1962.
2 *The Apocryphal New Testament,* M. R. James, trans. *Gospel of Thomas,* Greek Text A, 49.
3 Op. cit., 50.

CHAPTER 13: THE WEDDING IN CANA

1 See comment of the Douay Version, ad loc.
2 Gustaf Dalman in his study *Jesus-Jeshua,* Paul P. Levertolf, trans., states, "When one's mother is addressed as 'woman' it means a relinquishment of physical relationship," Op. cit., 202.

CHAPTER 14: "THE BRETHREN" OF JESUS

1 *The Aprocryphal New Testament.* M. N. James trans., 84.
2 George M. Lamsa, *The Peshitta,* loc. cit.

CHAPTER 15: MIRIAM AT THE CROSS

1 We note here the strong affirmation of the resurrection from the dead. This was a doctrine preached by the Pharisees and believed in by the majority of Jews. The Sadducees as we know from the New Testament denied the resurrection (Mk. 12:18).
2 Eusebius *Ecclesiastical History,* Book 3. (Baker, Grand Rapids, MI, 1955), chap. 20.

CHAPTER 16: MIRIAM IN THE UPPER ROOM

1 *Apocryphal New Testament.* The Assumption of the Virgin, Coptic Text, M. R. James, trans., 194-198.

CHAPTER 17: TRANSFORMATION OF MIRIAM INTO MARY

1 Apuleius, *Metamorphoses* Book 9, quoted by Miegge, The Virgin Mary, 69.
2 Ibid, 74. It is interesting to note that during Muhammad's lifetime the cult of Mary was already so strong in Arabia, that he thought the Christian Trinity consisted of Father, Son, and Mary (see appendix II).

3 Ibid., 61.
4 Ibid,. 78.

CHAPTER 18: THE IMMACULATE CONCEPTION

1 Origen, Homilia 17 in Lucam.
2 Augustine De Natura et Gratia cap. 36. Quoted by Miegge, op. cit., 110.
3 Bernard of Clairvaux, Epistula 174.
4 Calvini Tractatus theologici omnes, Geneva 1597, 358.

CHAPTER 19: THE ASSUMPTION OF MARY

1 Epiphanius Panarion 78:11,24.
2 Epistula ad Paulam et Eustochium. Miegge op. cit., 96.
3 Ascribed to Augustine, Liber de Assumptione, cap. 8.

CHAPTER 20: MARY THE CO-REDEMPTRESS

1 Roman Catholic theology does not admit the existence of new dogmas, but teaches that these are as old as the Church and were always believed by the faithful. What appears to be a "new dogma" is, they say, merely a development of that which was always there in "seed" form, and was inherent in "the deposit of faith or revelation."
2 W. Goosens, *De Cooperatione immediata Matris Redemptoris ad redemptionem objectivam.* Roschini: Mariologia II.
3 W. Goosens quoted by Miegge op. cit., 157.
4 Victor Buksbazen, *Miriam the Virgin of Nazareth*, chap. 6.
5 Roschini: Mariologia II, 158.
6 Hermann Volk: *Christus und Maria*, 22 (author's translation).
7 Roschini: op. cit., 291.

CHAPTER 21: MARIAN PIETY

1 Volk, *Christus und Maria*, 5-6.
2 Manual of our Lady of Perpetual Help, (New York, NY: 1880), 52–53.
3 Many authorities in the Church of Rome have been clamoring for years for a papal decree exalting Mary as Co-Redemptrix with Christ. Karl Adam, a renowned Roman Catholic theologian, in his book, *The Spirit of Catholicism*, writes that "belief in the universal intercessory mediatorship of Mary...is beginning to come ripe for definition." An

American Jesuit professor of Patristic Theology likewise predicts: "It may soon be defined as part and parcel of God's public revelation that in union with her Son the Virgin redeemed the world." Perhaps the greatest hurdle to the Second Vatican Council promulgating such a doctrine is the fact that it would be so much of an offense to Protestants that all their unity overtures to these "separated brethren" would be completely undermined. There is nothing to hinder Pope John XXIII, however, following the precedent established by former Pontiffs from announcing, *ex cathedra*, that the Virgin Mary is indeed Co-Redemptress with her Son of all the world. We do know that in his message to the International Marian Academy in 1961, the Pope declared: "We realize that Mariology must not go beyond truth as a result of false or immoderate boldness." But he was also quick to add, "It (Mariology) must not be restricted within too narrow limits in considering that special dignity proper to the Mother of God and to Alma Socia (Associate Virgin) of Christ the Redeemer." Stuart P. Garver, *Pope John and the Virgin Mary.* Christian Heritage, January 1963, 30-31.

APPENDIX I: MIRIAM IN THE TALMUD

[1] Tractate Kallah 18b—Dalman and Laible's *Jesus Christ in the Talmud*, 33.

[2] Victor Buksbazen, *The Gospel in the Feasts of Israel*, 73: "Nevertheless, the separation between believers and unbelievers was soon forced upon the Christians by violence and persecution. The first martyr for the faith was Stephen. Active persecution of Jewish believers, the vilification of the Person of the Lord Jesus, and changes in the liturgy, which contained direct or implicit denunciation of the believers in the Messiah Jesus, drove the Jewish Christians out of the Temple and from the synagogue."

[3] For a full discussion of the Ebionites and primitive Hebrew-Christianity see Jakob Jocz, *The Jewish People and Jesus Christ* (London:The Society for the Propagation of Christian Knowledge) 191-200.

[4] For a full discussion of this matter we refer to Dalman and Laible's *Jesus Christ in the Talmud*, 33-39.

[5] It is interesting to note how far, in our times, the pendulum has swung

the other way. Recently a reform rabbi in New York demanded that the New Testament be purged of "flaws" or "lies," because according to this rabbi, the New Testament, especially the Gospel of Matthew, was supposed to have anti-Semitic passages. "Let's Get Them to Correct New Testament: Rabbi." *The National Jewish Post and Opinion*, March 12, 1962.

6 Gustaf Dalman; op. cit., 8-9.

7 Any interested student may look up these passages in the excellent English translation of the Talmud published in 1961 by the Soncino Press in London, England, in the Index Volume under the subjects: Miriam, 259; Jesus, 207; and Jeshu, 467. See also Jakob Jocz, *The Jewish People and Jesus Christ,* 59-65.

8 See Rabbi Morris Goldman, M.A.D.H.L. *Jesus in the Jewish Tradition.* (MacMillan, 1950).

APPENDIX II: MIRIAM IN THE QUR'AN

1 *The Glorious Qur'an,* translated by M. M. Pickthall.

2 Eusebius, *Historia Ecclesiastica,* Book 6.

3 The Muslims claim to have the "authentic gospel" which they call *The Gospel according to St. Barnabas.* But even this "gospel" is almost unknown among them.

APPENDIX III: THE DEPOSIT OF FAITH

1 See *A Catholic Dictionary* third edition, D. Attwater, ed., 143.

2 Compare S. D. Benedict *Catholic Doctrine in the Bible*, 89-90.

BIBLIOGRAPHY

Aron, Robert. (1962). *Jesus of Nazareth, The Hidden Years*. New York, NY: W. Morrow.

Attwater, Donald, ed. (1961). *A Catholic Dictionary*, 3rd ed. New York, NY: MacMillan.

Benedict, Samuel D. (1930). *Catholic Doctrine in the Bible*. Chicago, IL: National Christian Association.

Berkouwer, G. C. *Recent Development in Roman Catholic Thought*. Grand Rapids, MI: Eerdmans.

Booth-Clibborn, Catherine. *Mary, the Mother of Our Lord*. London: Marshall, Morgan & Scott, Ltd.

Boyle, Isaac, trans., *Ecclesiastical History of Eusebius*. Grand Rapids, MI: Baker.

Box, G. H. (1919). *The Apocalypse of Abraham*. London: Society for the Promotion of Christian Knowledge (SPCK).

Burrows, Millar. (1955). *The Dead Sea Scrolls*. New York, NY: Viking.

Charles, R. H. (1902). *The Book of Jubilees or The Little Genesis*. London: SPCK.

Charles, R. H. (1918). *The Apocalypse of Baruch and the Assumption of Moses*. London: SPCK.

Charles, R. H. (1912). *The Book of Enoch*. London: SPCK.

Cohn, A. (1949). *Everyman's Talmud*. New York, NY: Dutton.

Dalman, Gustaf. A. W. Streane, trans. (1893). *Jesus Christ in the Talmud*. Cambridge: Deighton, Bell & Company.

Dalman, Gustaf. Paul P. Levertoff, trans. (1929). *Jesus-Jeshua*. London: SPCK.

Danby, Herbert, trans. *The Mishnah*. London: Oxford University.

Davis, John D. *Dictionary of the Bible*. Grand Rapids, MI: Baker.

Delitsch, Franz. (1901). *New Testament Edition in Hebrew*. London: British & Foreign Bible Society.

Devine, C. F. *Did Mary Have Other Children?* St. Alphonsus Seminary. Woodstock, Ontario: The League of St. Gerard.

Dickinson, G. Lowes. (1957). *The Greek View of Life*. Ann Arbor, MI: University of Michigan.

Edersheim, Alfred. (1876). *Sketches of Jewish Social Life in the Days of Christ*.

Edersheim, Alfred. (1885). *Prophecy in History*.

Edersheim, Alfred. (1856). *History of the Jewish Nation*.

Edersheim, Alfred. (1874). *The Temple*.

Edersheim, Alfred. *Third and Fourth Books of the Maccabees.* London: SPCK.

Epstein, I., ed. *The Talmud* (18 volumes) in English. London: Soncino.

Finkelstein, Louis. (1966). *The Pharisees.* Philadelphia, PA: Jewish Publication Society.

Finkelstein, Louis. (1949). *The Jews, Their History, Culture and Religion.* Philadelphia, PA: Jewish Publication Society.

Gafolo, Salvatore. (1961). *Mary in The Bible.* Milwaukee, WI: Bruce Publishing.

Ganzfried, S. and H. E. Goldin, trans. *Code of Jewish Law (Shulchan Aruch).*

Gaster, Theodore H., trans. (1956). *The Dead Sea Scriptures.* New York, NY: Doubleday.

Goldstein, Morris. (1950). *Jesus in the Jewish Tradition.* London: MacMillan.

Goodspeed, Edgar J. (1939). *The Apocrypha.* New York, NY: Random House; *The Apocrypha.* London: SPCK.

Grant, Michael. (1960). *The World of Rome.* Dublin: Mentor.

Graetz, Heinrich. (1891). *History of the Jews.* Philadelphia, PA: Jewish Publication Society.

Graves, Robert, trans. (1952). *The Golden Ass of Apuleius.* New York, NY: Pocket Books.

James, Montague R., trans. (1924). *The Lost Apocrypha of the Old Testament.* London: SPCK.

James, Montague R., trans. (1924). *The Apocryphal New Testament*

Jocz, Jakob. (1954). *The Jewish People and Jesus Christ* London: SPCK.

Johnson, Sherman E. (1957). *Jesus in His Homeland.* Philadelphia, PA: The Westminster Press.

Keith, Khodad E. (1959). The *Social Life of a Jew.* London: Church Missions to the Jews.

Keller, Werner. (1955). *The Bible as History.* London: Hodder & Stoughton.

Kinkead, Thomas L. (1891). *Catechism of Christian Doctrine.*

Klausner, Joseph. (1955). *The Messianic Idea in Israel.* New York, NY: MacMillan.

Lamsa, G. M., trans. (1967). *The Peshitta* (Syriac Bible). Philadelphia, PA: A.J. Holman.

LaSor, W. S. (1959). *Great Personalities of the Old Testament.* Westwood, NJ: Fleming H. Revell.

Marcus, Ralph, trans. (1943). *Josephus Works.* Cambridge, MA: Harvard University.

Metzger, Bruce M. (1957). *An Introduction to the Apocrypha.* New York, NY:

Oxford Press.

Miegge, Giovanni. (1950). *The Virgin Mary.* Philadelphia, PA: The Westminster Press.

Montefiore, C. G. and Loewe, H. *Anthology of Rabbinic Literature.* Philadelphia, PA: Jewish Publication Society.

Montefiore, C. G. (1930). *Rabbinical Literature and the Gospel Teachings.* London: MacMillan.

Moore, George Foot. (1927). *Judaism.* Cambridge, MA: Harvard University.

Neil, James, M.A., *Peeps into Palestine.* London: Henry E. Walter.

Oesterley, W. O. E. (1919). *The Sayings of the Jewish Fathers.* London: SPCK.

Oesterley, W. O. E. (1917). *The Wisdom of Solomon.* London: SPCK.

Oesterley, W. O. E. (1916). *The Wisdom of Ben-Sira.* London:SPCK.

Picthall, Muhammad M. (1930). *The Glorious Qur'an.* New York, NY: The New American Library.

Robertson, A. T. (1925). *The Mother of Jesus, Her Problems and Her Glory.* New York, NY: Doran.

Salkinson, Isaac, trans. (1898). *New Testament in Hebrew. Greek New Testament* (Textus Receptus). London: British and Foreign Bible Society, London.

Schlink, M. Basilea (1960). *Maria, Der Weg der Mutter des Herrn.* Darmstadt-Eberstadt: Oekumenische Marienschwesternschaft.

Manual of Our Lady of Perpetual Help. (1880). New York, NY: Sullivan.

Thompson, J. A. (1962). *Archeology and the Old Testament.* Grand Rapids, MI: Eerdmans.

Thompson, J. A. (1960). *Archeology and the New Testament.* Grand Rapids, MI: Eerdmans.

Thompson, J. A. (1959). *Archeology in the Pre-New Testament Centuries.* Grand Rapids, MI: Eerdmans.

Twilley, L. D. (1959). *The Origin and Transmission of the New Testament.* Grand Rapids, MI: Eerdmans.

Vergil, *The Aeneid.* Bantam: New York, NY.

Volk, Hermann. (1939). *Christus und Maria.* Westfalen: Verlag Aschendorff, Muenster.

Whiston, William, trans. (1737). *Josephus Works.*